Praise for
*Something Needs to Change*

"Rugged. Authentic. Gritty. Real. Worshipful. There are no other books like this one. I always pick up David's books with a sense of excitement and, quite honestly, apprehension—because I know that areas of compromise and complacency in my life are going to be exposed. But this book exceeded even my high expectations, for which I am grateful. And so will you be. As David writes, it's time to run, not walk. Let's go."

> —J. D. Greear, president of the Southern Baptist
> Convention

"Extraordinary and challenging. I've just never read a book like this before. I am so moved. Bring your full heart to this story and watch how God opens your eyes, changes your mind, and broadens the dreams you have for your life."

> —Annie F. Downs, bestselling author of *100 Days
> to Brave* and *Remember God*

"If you dare to read this book, you might just have an unexpected encounter with Jesus that leaves you weeping on the floor, as David's experience did. Something changes within us when the seemingly overwhelming needs of the world present themselves simply in the life of a single person. Ultimately, I pray your compassion will be transformed to action."

> —Santiago "Jimmy" Mellado, president and CEO
> of Compassion International

"Grippingly vulnerable, humble, and unforgettable, this book holds the catalytic power for life change. Platt leads you on an astonishingly transparent interior journey of his heart and mind, demonstrating transformative, cruciform discipleship in real time."

—ANN VOSKAMP, author of the *New York Times* bestsellers *The Broken Way* and *One Thousand Gifts*

"I wholeheartedly recommend *Something Needs to Change*. God spoke to me through it, and that's the best I can say about any book."

—RANDY ALCORN, founder of Eternal Perspective Ministries and author of *If God Is Good*

"Riveting. Wrecking. Raw. *Something Needs to Change* is a harrowing physical and spiritual journey through areas of deep need, tenuous terrain, and spiritual oppression, as well as a beautiful, hope-filled invitation to come penetrate the present darkness with the light of Christ. This resource will reawaken your faith, reorient you to the calling of Christ, and remind you of the importance and value of your role in God's redemption story."

—LOUIE GIGLIO, pastor of Passion City Church, founder of Passion Conferences, and author of *Not Forsaken*

"*Something Needs to Change* will bring you to a crossroads in your faith: Who and what are you living for? If heaven and hell are real and there are billions of people who don't know Jesus, then what are you going to do about it? Prepare to be challenged."

—JENNIE ALLEN, author of *Nothing to Prove* and founder of IF:Gathering

"Few of us will trek the Himalayas, let alone face the type of suffering and need that people experience daily in that region and around the world. In *Something Needs to Change*, David Platt serves all of us by exposing us to the stories and lives of those he encountered during his personal journey through this mountainous region. We all want our lives to count, and Platt helps guide us toward a vision for just that."

—TRILLIA NEWBELL, author of *Sacred Endurance, Enjoy,* and the children's book *God's Very Good Idea*

"The message of David Platt's new book, *Something Needs to Change,* could not be more timely. I have witnessed the kind of heartbreaking situations David describes, and I agree with him that what needs to change to address such suffering is *us*. It is only when we yield to the transformative work of the Holy Spirit in us—to make us more like Jesus—that we can participate in the transformation God is doing around the world. I know personally how much joy can be found in allowing Christ to work in and through me this way. Read this book, join the journey, and be open to the change God wants to do in you!"

—EDGAR SANDOVAL SR., president of World Vision U.S.

# SOMETHING NEEDS TO CHANGE

# DAVID PLATT

*New York Times* bestselling author of *Radical*

# SOMETHING NEEDS TO CHANGE

## An Urgent Call to Make Your Life Count

MULTNOMAH

All Scripture quotations, unless otherwise noted, are taken from the Christian Standard Bible®, copyright © 2017 by Holman Bible Publishers. Used by permission. Christian Standard Bible® and CSB® are federally registered trademarks of Holman Bible Publishers. The quoted words in the prayer on page 112 and those marked (ESV) are taken from the ESV® Bible (The Holy Bible, English Standard Version®), copyright © 2001 by Crossway, a publishing ministry of Good News Publishers. Used by permission. All rights reserved.

Details in some anecdotes and stories have been changed to protect the identities of the persons involved.

The author's royalties from this book will go toward promoting the glory of Christ in all nations.

Published in the United States by Multnomah, an imprint of Random House, a division of Penguin Random House LLC. Published in association with Yates & Yates, www.yates2.com.

Multnomah® and its mountain colophon are registered trademarks of Penguin Random House LLC.

Originally published in hardcover in the United States as *Something Needs to Change: A Call to Make Your Life Count in a World of Urgent Need* by Multnomah, an imprint of Random House, a division of Penguin Random House LLC, in 2019.

Paperback ISBN 978-0-7352-9143-0

The Library of Congress has cataloged the hardcover edition as follows:
Names: Platt, David.
Title: Something needs to change : a call to make your life count in a world of urgent need / David Platt.
Description: First Edition. | Colorado Springs : Multnomah, 2019. |
    Includes bibliographical references.
Identifiers: LCCN 2019000481 | ISBN 9780735291416 (hardcover) |
    ISBN 9780735291423 (electronic)
Subjects: LCSH: Church work with the poor. | Change—Religious aspects—Christianity.
Classification: LCC BV639.P6 P545 2019 | DDC 261.8/325—dc23
LC record available at https://lccn.loc.gov/2019000481

Printed in the United States of America on acid-free paper

waterbrookmultnomah.com

9 8 7 6 5 4 3 2 1

First Trade Paperback Edition

*Interior book design by Karen Sherry*

Special Sales
Most Multnomah books are available at special quantity discounts when purchased in bulk by corporations, organizations, and special-interest groups. Custom imprinting or excerpting can also be done to fit special needs. For information, please email specialmarketscms@penguinrandomhouse.com.

To "Aaron" and all those he represents.

# Contents

# Author's Note

In some parts of the world, following Jesus is a dangerous business. The trek described in these pages details events seen and heard through multiple trips on Himalayan trails, where the gospel is not always welcome. Everything and everyone described in this book is real, but for security reasons, key names, places, times, and other details have been altered to protect the people involved.

# SOMETHING
# NEEDS
# TO
# CHANGE

# Why the Tears?

lone in a guesthouse at the base of the Himalayas, I found myself on my knees, face to the floor, sobbing. Scattered around me was the evidence of my past week—a backpack, trekking poles, hiking boots. I was fresh off a weeklong journey through some of the highest mountains in the world and only hours from a flight home to the States.

But I hadn't planned on ending my trip with out-of-control tears.

Up to that day, I could count on one hand the number of times I'd cried in my adult life. The last time I'd wept was the day I received the phone call that my dad had died of a sudden heart attack. But this day in an Asian guesthouse was different. This time I wasn't weeping because *I* was missing someone or even something. Instead, I was crying uncontrollably because of what *others*—men, women, and children I'd met the past week—were missing. Things like water, food, family members . . . freedom and hope. I so longed for them to have these things that I couldn't help it. I fell to the floor sobbing, and the flood of tears wouldn't stop.

## What We Need

Looking back on that day in the guesthouse, I wonder why being so overwhelmed for others in need has been uncommon for me. I think of all the church services I've been in week after week, year after year, talking and hearing about the needs of people all over the world. I think of all the sermons I've preached about serving those in need. I even think about the books I've written, including *Radical*—for crying out loud—a book about laying down our lives in love for Christ and the world around us. So why has it been rare for me to be so moved by the needs of others that I have fallen on my face before God and wept?

I don't think this question is just for me. When I think of all those church services, I recall very few instances when other Christians and I have wept together for people who were missing water, food, family, freedom, or hope. Why is a scene like that so uncommon among us?

It makes me wonder if we've lost our capacity to weep. It makes me wonder if we have subtly, dangerously, and almost unknowingly guarded our lives, our families, and even our churches from truly being affected by God's words to us in a world of urgent spiritual and physical needs around us. We talk a lot about the need to *know* what we believe in our heads, yet I wonder if we have forgotten to *feel* what we believe in our hearts. How else are we to explain our ability to sit in services where we sing songs and hear sermons celebrating how Jesus is the hope of the world, yet rarely (if ever) fall on our faces weeping for those who don't have this hope and then take action to make this hope known to them?

Why today do we seem to be so far from the way of Jesus? Jesus wept over those in need. He was moved with compassion for the crowds. He lived and loved to bring healing and comfort to the broken. He died for the sins of the world. So why are those of us who carry his Spirit not moved and compelled in the same way? Surely God didn't design the gospel of Jesus to be confined to our minds and mouths in the church, yet disconnected from our emotions and actions in the world.

*Surely something needs to change.*

But how? When I found myself face first on that guesthouse floor, it wasn't because I'd heard a new fact about suffering in the world or even made a new discovery in God's Word. On the long flight to Asia, I had actually written an entire sermon on poverty and oppression, complete with staggering numbers concerning the poor and oppressed in the world today. And I had written it from an emotionally well-guarded, frighteningly coldhearted perspective. Somehow, staring at statistics on poverty and even studying the Bible had left my soul unscathed. But when I came face to face with men, women, and children in urgent spiritual and physical need, the wall in my heart was breached. And I wept.

Clearly, the change we need won't happen simply by our seeing more facts or listening to more sermons (or even preaching them, for that matter). What we need is not an explanation of the

Word and the world that puts more information in our heads; we need an experience with the Word *in the world* that penetrates the recesses of our hearts. We need to dare to come face to face with desperate need in the world around us and ask God to do a work deep within us that we could never manufacture, manipulate, or make happen on our own.

This is my prayer for the pages ahead.

## A Risk

I've taken a different approach in writing this book. I'm most naturally a preacher who makes use of exposition and explanation to communicate his points. But as I've mentioned, I don't think we need more exposition and explanation. I think we need an experience—an encounter that takes exposed and explained truth to a deeper level in our hearts than it would ever go otherwise.

So in this book I want to take off my preacher hat and invite you to experience a trek with me through some of the highest mountains of Asia. I invite you to eat what I ate, drink what I drank, see the faces I saw, touch the people I touched, and, in all of this, feel the emotions I felt. In the end, I want to consider with you how to transfer this trek through the Himalayas into everyday life where we live. I want to imagine with you what might happen if we let the gospel penetrate beyond our heads to our hearts in a way that dramatically changes the course of our lives, families, and churches in the world.

I believe that in using my mountain trek as the setting for this book, there's risk involved—for both you and me. For me the risk is leaving the security of the platform where I normally preach, and even coming out from behind the desk where I normally write, to share some struggles I have with things I preach and truths I believe. By inviting you on these trails, I want to open my personal thoughts to you, and I don't want to hide my most profound questions from you.

For example, if the gospel is really true and God is really good, then where are the truth and goodness of God amid extreme poverty and pain? And where are his peace and protection for the oppressed and exploited?

And what of life beyond this world? In a universe governed by a good God, is hell really a place and does it actually last forever? If it really exists and really won't end, then why are so many people born into an earthly hell only to move on to an eternal one? And will billions of individuals who don't believe in Jesus really go there, even if they never had a chance to hear about him?

It may surprise you to find that even a pastor like me, who absolutely believes in the truth and reliability of Scripture, still wrestles with questions like these. I do. And I know it's one thing to ask these questions behind a podium in a comfortable building on a Sunday morning, but a whole other thing to ask these questions when you're standing on a mountainside with a man whose wife and kids died in a matter of hours of a preventable disease because no medicine was available. Or when you're looking into the face of a twelve-year-old girl who wants sex with you, because that's what she was sold and enslaved to do since she was ten. Or when you're watching a body physically burn on a funeral pyre and you know that person never even heard of Jesus.

I want to take a risk in sharing a more behind-the-scenes look into what happens when a preacher and author with three seminary degrees has his deepest convictions rocked by darkness in the world around him and finds himself asking honestly, *Is Jesus really the hope of the world after all?*

I believe there's risk here for you, too. Now, just so you know, I am saving you a lot of risk by writing this book. You don't have to risk flying on a helicopter into a remote part of the world where if something bad happens to you, you're virtually disconnected from outside communication and days away from getting any help. I'm saving you the risk of crossing suspended bridges and hiking narrow trails where one slip might mean tumbling to your death. You don't have to worry about altitude sickness, amebic dysentery, traveler's diarrhea, cyclospora, giardia, malaria, hepatitis, or . . . I think you get the point. Suffice to say that "you're welcome" for saving you from all these risks!

But you can't avoid all risk by joining me on this trek. I had no idea what would happen in my life after a week on those trails. So by inviting you to come with me into these mountains, I'm asking you to open yourself to the possibility that the way you view your life, your family, your church, or your future might not be the same when you return. I don't know if you'll find yourself on the floor weeping uncontrollably. But I do hope that you'll find yourself unguarded. Unfiltered. And ultimately open to a whole new world of what God wants to do in and through your life.

So if you're up for that journey, I invite you to turn the page. Because something needs to change.

# Preparation

*E*ven a short trip into the Himalayas takes preparation. A small team and I would be hiking through mountain trails at elevations higher than any of us had ever experienced (unless flying in a plane). Almost unimaginably, more than one hundred peaks in the Himalayas soar above twenty-four thousand feet. This mountain range spans five different countries—Nepal, India, Bhutan, China, and Pakistan—six if you count Tibet.

I knew the trip would be physically demanding, so I trained

by doing CrossFit, walking on an incline treadmill every morning for months, and hiking to the crest of the highest mountain near me. Unfortunately, that mountain soared a mere thousand feet above sea level. That's not even a hill in the Himalayas.

In addition to physical training, packing for the trek required careful planning. Each member of the team would need to carry all his own gear—that is, no assistance from Sherpas or yaks. So the goal was to hold the weight of all our clothing and miscellaneous gear to no more than twenty pounds. Since at the highest elevation we would sleep with temperatures well below freezing, this meant toting a down sleeping bag rated to fifteen degrees.

Also going in the backpack:
- a change of clothes for midway through the trek
- a small towel and minimal toiletries
- a hat, sunscreen, and sunglasses for daytime hiking
- a headlamp for hiking at night
- a filtered water bottle
- snacks (not a lot of vending machines along the trail)
- a Bible and a journal

## Backstory

Just how did I end up on this trek? Primarily, it was because of a meeting one day with a guy named Aaron who is now a good friend of mine.

I first met Aaron when he visited the church where I was the pastor. He introduced himself to me after a worship service and told me he lived in Asia, but that was all. I didn't see him again for a couple more years. During those years, God led my wife, Heather, and me to pursue adopting a child from the same country where Aaron lives. We had heard about living conditions there for many children, including young girls who were enslaved for sex, so we decided to bring one of these children into our family.

We started the adoption process, and night after night, Heather and I gathered together with our two boys at the time and prayed for their little sister-to-be. Everything went smoothly, and our next step was to be matched with a specific little girl. Then, without warning, this country closed down adoption for foreigners. Our hearts were devastated.

That Christmas was a sad one for us, so I wrote a poem for Heather, my attempt to express the heaviness we both felt. I detailed all the struggles we had been through, the deep longings we had experienced to have this special girl be part of our family. Expressing these feelings in the voice of the child we'd never meet, I ended the poem with these lines:

> So let love hope and let love plead,
> To God on behalf of a prospective little daughter-to-be.
> And regardless of whether or not my parents one day
>     you'll be,
> Please promise that your family will never stop praying
>     for me.

This country remained closed, but Heather and I trusted that God had put this place on our hearts for a purpose. So when we weren't able to adopt, the next time Aaron was passing through and said hello after another church service, I said, "Can you and I meet together in my office tomorrow morning?"

The next day Aaron shared with me how the living conditions for many children in his country were indeed dire and that more girls than either of us could (or would want to) imagine were enslaved for sex. As we talked, he invited me to join him on a trek, and it was a no-brainer—*I was in.*

## Saying Goodbye

I love visiting other parts of the world to share the gospel, but I hate saying goodbye. Since I travel overseas a fair amount and these trips aren't always to destinations the US State Department recommends for travel, I try to keep a letter updated to Heather and our kids just in case something were to happen to me. Needless to say, writing that letter is never enjoyable, but it's a precious reminder of how much you love those closest to you.

On this trip I was encouraged that two men would accompany me. First, there was Chris, a lifelong friend I've known since childhood. We now work together in an organization called Radical (https://radical.net), a global ministry and giving platform aimed at serving the church and spreading the gospel on the front lines of urgent need around the world.

Our second trekking teammate was a man I'd just met. He goes by the nickname of Sigs, and his role would be to document the trip with photography and video. I learned quickly that Sigs is an adventurous soul who has a special talent for asking questions that really make me think. In addition to carrying his personal effects in his pack, he would also lug the camera gear, complete with extra batteries. Finding electrical outlets to recharge equipment in the Himalayan backcountry . . . well, good luck with that.

## Good News?

En route, as the plane sailed through one time zone after another, I tried to sleep. I read my Bible and jotted some notes in my journal. I started missing Heather and the kids. I prayed silently for them in a deep way, asking God for an extra measure of his protection and provision for them while I'd be gone.

I also had an interesting conversation with a seatmate. His name was Charles and I learned that he was from the Congo. He also was blind. Telling me some of his story, he shared that his blindness was the result of a botched eye surgery. As we became better acquainted, I told him the purpose of my trip and had an opportunity to share the gospel with him.

Charles was not thrilled to find out I was a follower of Jesus. He told me how his people had been hurt and harmed by some missionaries from Europe who, according to him, in the name of Christ had done disastrous things in his country. As a result, Charles's view of Jesus was significantly—and sadly—distorted.

It humbled me to hear that his experience with the "good news," as he had heard it, was not good at all. Apparently, it's possible for various misrepresentations of the gospel to actually drive people further away from God.

I did my best to convince Charles that the true Jesus is nothing like those people who had hurt him, but he seemed unconvinced. Later I scribbled reflections in my journal about my desire to never misrepresent Jesus:

*O God, that's the last thing I want to do. Please help me, help us, to give people an accurate picture of you that draws them to you, not pushes them from you.*

# *Day 1:* Arrival

## Excited but Tired

Thirty hours in coach on an airplane wears you out. It's late in the evening when we groggily step off our final plane flight out of Europe into Asia. As the plane taxis toward the terminal, Chris says with a yawn, "All I want is a place to stretch out and lie down!"

"I hear you," I answer. I look across the aisle at Sigs, who, after he closed his tray and put his seat upright, had fallen back asleep. Yup, we're all tired.

We gather our carry-ons, and as we exit the Jetway, new sights, smells, and sounds bombard our senses. Most everyone around us is speaking a different language. Many of the women are wearing long, casual, colorful outfits with a head covering. Some of the men sport long, baggy, double-breasted shirts over matching pants. The airport restaurants give off a uniquely pungent aroma of spice and seasoning. Exhausted as we are, we still quickly realize we're not in Kansas anymore.

Somewhat disoriented, our anxiety rises because we're not sure exactly what to do or where to go. The airport signage is puzzling, written in another language and sometimes translated into English in a way that doesn't quite make sense.

When in doubt, you go with the herd, so we hoist our packs and follow our fellow passengers toward customs. With groans we see there's a long line, which we discover is scarcely moving. As we creep along we exchange glances of frustration. I suppose there's some subtle arrogance in our thoughts as our facial expressions and body language say, *I can count so many ways this system could be more efficient.* Doesn't matter. There's nothing to do but stand and shuffle.

After an hour-long wait provides us with plenty of time to stretch our legs, we hand our passports to an agent who glances at each of our photos and then at our faces before verifying the validity of our visas.

"Why are you visiting our country?" he asks.

"We want to trek through the mountains," I answer.

He nods, stamps each passport, and waves us through.

Since we are carrying everything we need in our backpacks, there's no other baggage to retrieve. As we exit the front door of the terminal building, Aaron is waiting. I greet him with a handshake and hug, then introduce him to Sigs and Chris.

"You look very tired," Aaron says with a grin. We nod in agreement. He leads us to his small van. After we climb in—sitting again actually feels good already—he starts the engine, pulls out into traffic, and says, "Let's get you to the guesthouse, where you can get some sleep."

## Crazy Traffic

In this large Asian city, even though it's several hours after sundown, the streets are clogged with traffic. I mean *traffic*—every imaginable type of two-, three-, and four-wheeled vehicle, from pedal bikes to rickshaws to scooters to cars to buses to semitrucks. *Chaos!*

Aaron seems unconcerned with the near collisions that occur by the minute. He weaves the van along, often sounding his horn. Horns seem to have their own language, as drivers continually honk to communicate with others. All of us are wide awake now since this makes rush hour at home look like child's play. It's impossible to figure out the traffic laws (or if such laws even exist). The stoplights seem more like suggestions than requirements. Some intersections simply involve a multitude of vehicles arriving from every direction, converging in the middle, then slowly weaving in and out to the desired street.

In addition to the mayhem, I notice my eyes stinging slightly from the pollution, with clouds of exhaust and dust rising from semi-paved streets. Some of the residents riding the two-wheelers are wearing surgical masks to screen out some of the dirty air.

We pass by a motorcycle driven by a man who has a child in his lap, a woman (presumably his wife) sitting behind him side-saddle and holding a baby, and then two other kids squeezed in behind her. Who needs a minivan when a motorcycle will suffice?

After an hour in the hectic traffic, we arrive at the guest-house—ah, at last the opportunity to stretch full out and sleep. We drop our packs in a room.

Before we crash for the night, Aaron gathers us for some instruction and words of encouragement: "I know these plane rides have exhausted you, and the thought of one more flight in the morning is not very appealing. But trust me. The flight tomorrow is one you will never forget!"

## I Must Write This Down

I make my way to my guesthouse room, a quaint setup with a single bed and side table. A small window opens to the outside, letting a cool breeze blow gently into the room. With the soft wind comes steady noise from the street as men and women, cars and motorcycles, continue on in what seems like never-ending activity.

As I climb into bed, I pull the journal from my pack. When I was younger, a mentor of mine encouraged me to journal as part of my relationship with God. I began writing out reflections on what God was teaching me in his Word and how I saw him working in my life and the world around me. Those reflections would inevitably turn into prayers of praise and thanks to him, petitions for my life, and intercession for others. I can't say I've journaled every day since that time, but I've done so off and on for many years and almost every day over recent years.

So even though I can barely hold my eyes open, I read these verses from Scripture (in my daily Bible reading, I was in this part of Luke) and journal along the way:

> In the fifteenth year of the reign of Tiberius Caesar, while
> Pontius Pilate was governor of Judea, Herod was tetrarch
> of Galilee, his brother Philip tetrarch of the region of
> Iturea and Trachonitis, and Lysanias tetrarch of Abilene,
> during the high priesthood of Annas and Caiaphas, God's
> word came to John the son of Zechariah in the wilderness.
> He went into all the vicinity of the Jordan, proclaiming a
> baptism of repentance for the forgiveness of sins, as it is
> written in the book of the words of the prophet Isaiah:
>
> > A voice of one crying out in the wilderness:
> > Prepare the way for the Lord;
> > make his paths straight!
> > Every valley will be filled,
> > and every mountain and hill will be made low;
> > the crooked will become straight,
> > the rough ways smooth,
> > and everyone will see the salvation of God. (3:1–6)

I write in my journal,

*Talk about hope. Valleys filled, the crooked made straight, the rough made smooth, and everyone seeing the salvation of God. These words from Isaiah spoken thousands of years before find fulfillment in the coming of Jesus. He's the hope to whom all of history has been pointing.*

Reading more in Luke:

He then said to the crowds who came out to be baptized by him, "Brood of vipers! Who warned you to flee from the coming wrath? Therefore produce fruit consistent with repentance. And don't start saying to yourselves, 'We have Abraham as our father,' for I tell you that God is able to raise up children for Abraham from these stones. The ax is already at the root of the trees. Therefore, every tree that doesn't produce good fruit will be cut down and thrown into the fire." (verses 7–9)

*Repentance is far more important than religion. God makes clear that we can't rest in religion devoid of repentance. And true repentance is evident in the fruit of our lives.*

"What then should we do?" the crowds were asking him. He replied to them, "The one who has two shirts must share with someone who has none, and the one who has food must do the same."

Tax collectors also came to be baptized, and they asked him, "Teacher, what should we do?"

He told them, "Don't collect any more than what you have been authorized."

Some soldiers also questioned him, "What should we do?"

He said to them, "Don't take money from anyone by force or false accusation, and be satisfied with your wages." (verses 10–14)

*Repentance leads to a changed way of life. Repentance requires change.*

Now the people were waiting expectantly, and all of them were questioning in their hearts whether John might be the Messiah. John answered them all, "I baptize you with water, but one who is more powerful than I am is coming. I am not worthy to untie the strap of his sandals. He will baptize you with the Holy Spirit and fire. His winnowing shovel is in his hand to clear his threshing floor and gather the wheat into his barn, but the chaff he will burn with fire that never goes out." Then, along with many other exhortations, he proclaimed good news to the people. (verses 15–18)

*Clearly, the good news—the gospel—also involves bad news, a warning of coming judgment, even unquenchable fire. Lord,*

*help me to understand this gospel. To truly*
*believe what it means that your wrath is*
*real, and coming, for all who do not repent*
*and believe in Jesus. I don't think I even know*
*how to understand—or embrace—this truth.*
*I find it much easier to believe that your mercy*
*is real, and coming, for all who repent and*
*believe in Jesus.*

I fall asleep with my journal and Bible on my chest.

## Reflections

Because this book is intended to be an experience on these Himalayan trails, I will include a few questions at the end of each day of the trek to help you make the most of your own journey. So picture yourself at the end of this day lying down on a guesthouse bed (then starting tomorrow, in a cold sleeping bag), as you reflect on these questions and jot down any other thoughts or prayers that come to mind.

What would make you most nervous about going on a trek like this? What would make you most excited?

What about the gospel is hardest for you to understand?

# *Day 2:* A Long Way to Go Before Dark

## At the Ends of the Earth

The next morning, we arrive early at a ramshackle hangar. There are four in addition to me: Sigs, Chris, Aaron, and Nabin, who was born in this country and now works with Aaron. He will serve as our translator with people we meet along the way.

Aaron pulls us all together and says, "We're at close to five thousand feet above sea level right now, but we're about to ascend to about thirteen thousand feet. So I'd highly suggest you take this altitude medicine before we take off."

He hands a pill to each of us, and taking his word seriously, we all pop the pills and wash them down with swigs from our water bottles.

As we walk together toward the waiting chopper, I am nervous. I remember the one helicopter ride I've taken before. I had been invited to preach in Hawaii (not a hard invitation to accept, by the way), and on one day when Heather and I had some free time, we went on a helicopter tour through the mountains. While she relished looking out the window at the waterfalls, I looked at the bag in my lap, waiting to receive the lunch I'd eaten earlier. It was not a good experience.

The pilot walks over to us and gives instructions, mainly about avoiding being hit by the rotors: "Always approach and depart from the helicopter in the front, where I can see you," he says. "Walk in a low crouch with your head down and your gear secure at all times. Don't hold anything above eye level, because it may blow away. And if it does blow away, let it go. It's not worth losing your arm to keep your hat."

"Finally," he says with a look on his face that indicates he's seen one too many people try this, "please don't stop to take a selfie under the rotors when they're running right above you. Just get on or off the aircraft." Slowly, we each put our phone in a pocket.

"Once you're in your seat, buckle up tight and enjoy the ride." He concludes, "If there's an emergency at any point, just wait to follow my lead."

Sobered by the fact that an emergency is possible, we timidly gather for a picture in front of the helicopter (before the rotors start!). After the picture, we load our backpacks into the cages affixed to the side of the aircraft, then climb into our seats and buckle in. The pilot starts the rotors turning, and the noise of the chopper consumes the cabin. It is virtually impossible now to hear someone talking, so each of us is alone with his own thoughts.

We lift slowly off the ground and quickly see a dreamlike scene. Now we're above all the noise, dust, and chaotic traffic, and passing below us is an intricate maze of white, yellow, and orange buildings. Stretching as far as we can see is a massive urban jungle, home to millions of people here at the foot of the Himalayas. Before long, we rise above what the locals call "the hills"—mountain peaks of six, eight, and ten thousand feet, which would be noteworthy mountains most anywhere else in the world. But not here.

As we escape the haze from the city, we see firsthand why those previous peaks are called hills. Suddenly, mountains appear that seem to soar above the sky itself. They are so high that you crane your neck to get a glimpse of their peaks. The scenery is breathtaking. Below is a vivid green valley, like a river of lush forest and farmland winding through the surrounding mountains. But you cannot keep your eyes away for long from the towering peaks ahead, their snowcaps like a crown of white jewels gleaming in the morning sun.

A smile breaks on my face. I am like a little kid who gets an unexpected present. These majestic mountains are now face to face. I consider pulling out my phone and snapping a photo, but I know it wouldn't do *this* justice. So I just sit and gaze in awe.

For the next thirty minutes, the helicopter glides through the halls of giants. I've heard of mountains like Everest, Annapurna, Manaslu, and Lhotse, but now I'm seeing the likes of them. I'm overwhelmed by both their majesty and the vulnerability they create in me. *This is high-risk flying; if we have trouble, it's over for us.* My feelings remind me of being on a raft and floating a little too far out on the ocean: for a few seconds, you feel helpless, until you can paddle closer to shore. But the fear while flying up these valleys in between these monstrous mountains lasts longer than a few seconds. I pray silently for our safety, realizing that my feelings of helplessness and vulnerability aren't going away anytime soon.

I'm comforted when I think of Psalm 65:

O God of our salvation,
　the hope of all the ends of the earth
　　and of the farthest seas;
　the one who by his strength established the mountains,
　　being girded with might;
　who stills the roaring of the seas,
　　the roaring of their waves,
　　the tumult of the peoples,
　so that those who dwell at the ends of the earth are
　　　in awe at your signs. (verses 5–8, ESV)

That last line says it all. I feel like I'm there—literally at the ends of the earth—and, indeed, I'm in awe. And I feel calmer now, reminded that my life is in the hands of the One who "established the mountains."

---

As the half-hour trip comes to a close, the helicopter circles and lands on a small but level plateau in a place called Bumthang. Eager to begin his return trip, the pilot keeps the rotors turning. "Climb out, grab your gear, and go to the side," he yells.

One by one, in a crouch and with heads down, we walk away from the chopper, clutching our backpacks. Once we're all to safety, we watch the big bird lift off and fly down the valley, quickly disappearing from sight. The sound of the helicopter vanishes, replaced by silence. We stand still, totally captivated by the grandeur that surrounds us.

"What do you think?" Aaron breaks the silence with a knowing grin.

This preacher is not often speechless, but in this moment I am.

## Omelets and Chai

I'm not quiet for long, though, after I feel a chilly, biting wind, and say, "I think I'm cold! Really cold!"

The heated cockpit of the helicopter had shielded us from realizing what was happening in flight. The temperature had dropped from mildly cool to freezing cold. We should have also noticed that the higher we'd climbed, the more snow covered the ground.

"Yes, it's cold!" Aaron says with a laugh. "About minus-ten degrees Celsius—or fourteen degrees Fahrenheit!"

As my feet disappear and I sink to my shins into a sea of

spotless white snow, I'm hoping my boots really are waterproof. I'm also glad I'm wearing layers.

Here's how all of us are dressed:

- lower body: wool socks, long johns, and waterproof pants
- upper body: base undershirt, long-sleeve shirt, down jacket, and a hard shell to keep us dry from snow and rain
- head and hands: toboggan cap and gloves

With wisps of white puffing from our mouths, we hoist our packs and walk for two hundred yards to a nearby village teahouse. It's a brown wooden building with two small rooms: one with a table and stools, the other the kitchen. The teahouse is not that warm—its only heat comes from the kitchen fire—but it's a welcome shelter from the wind.

Once we're inside and seated around the table, the teahouse host greets us. Aaron orders some bread and an omelet, which here is a flattened egg, for each of us. As we wait, the host serves us masala tea (what Westerners call chai). Some people love it, and others don't. Count me in the latter category, but at this point I'll drink anything that's hot.

While we wait for our food, Aaron sets the stage for the trek. "Okay," he starts, "I'm really excited for your time on these trails. When I first decided to invite visitors up here, honestly, I was hesitant because this place is not for everyone. You will be shocked by some of what you see. But there are some unique things that happen in your heart when you're in these mountains, so I'm really glad you came."

As we sit and sip our tea, Aaron tells us about his first trip into the Himalayas. "Twenty years ago I came here with some college buddies. We just wanted to hike, take it all in, and be mountain hippies for a while. I started trekking up the mountain, but at our first rest stop, I saw some human physical and spiritual need that I'd never encountered before. I'll share more of the details later, but I was so stunned by what I'd seen that I couldn't sleep. I cried all night. The next morning, I told my friends I could not go any farther. I grabbed my pack and hiked back down the mountain. I wasn't sure what, but I knew I had to do something to help these people. It's a long story, but I've been working ever since to meet those needs with the hope of Jesus."

"Can you tell us a little of what you saw that made such a huge impression?" Sigs asks.

"Sure. The region we are in right now includes about nine million people. Out of that nine million, there are probably less than one hundred followers of Jesus. The reality is, most people here have never even heard of Jesus. This area is the birthplace of both Hinduism and Buddhism, and Christianity is hardly found anywhere."

"That's amazing," Chris says. "To think that after two thousand years, the gospel still hasn't come to people in these villages."

"That's the spiritual condition," Aaron says. "The people are also severely impoverished and disadvantaged. When I first came to these villages, I found that half the children were dying before their eighth birthday. Many weren't making it to their first."

*Half the children?* All of us are shaking our heads. I think about my kids—Caleb, Joshua, Mara, and Isaiah. I love each of them so much. I can't imagine losing two of them. That would be like Caleb or Joshua already dead and Mara or Isaiah dying any day now. One of my greatest fears is losing one of my children—I can't comprehend that actually being an expectation.

Our teahouse host brings our food, carefully setting a plate for each of us. But we hesitate to eat, still sobered by Aaron's words about the children. I don't have much appetite.

"You all need to eat," he says, "and I'll share more later. I just want you to be prepared for what you'll see. There's a lot of need here."

Following his advice, we all force down our eggs and some bread.

Aaron is right. None of us realize what we're about to face in the first village we will walk through.

## Blindness

"Put on your sunglasses," Aaron says as we shoulder our packs outside the teahouse. He points to the blue sky and the blazing sun. "With the way the sun is shining on this snow up here, without sunglasses you'll go blind before too long."

"Are you serious, Aaron?" I ask.

"Yeah, it's called snow blindness, sort of like sunburn in your eyes. And just like sunburn, by the time you notice the symptoms, it's too late. You can get blind spots or go completely blind for a day or two . . . or permanently."

With the others, I slip the shades over my eyes as we start walking down the trail. I use the word *trail* loosely, because it feels more like we are making our own path through the snow. But it's magnificent. We are surrounded on all sides by snow-covered peaks.

The mountain on our right is about twenty-seven thousand feet. To provide some perspective, we're hiking at around thirteen thousand feet, which is slightly lower than the height of Pikes Peak in Colorado. So right next to us, we're looking at a mountain that is like Pikes Peak stacked on top of another Pikes Peak!

After hiking up and down several small rises, in about five hundred yards we come upon a village with only a few homes. As we enter the village, a man steps out of his house. He's wearing a tattered beige shirt and a torn brown jacket with holes that no doubt prevent it from fulfilling its purpose. His jet-black hair, gray beard, and rough bronze skin look like they've not been washed for weeks. But none of these attributes are what sticks out about this man. I notice that he's missing an eye.

Aaron greets him in the local language, and the man, extremely soft spoken, mumbles a response, looking down with his one eye.

"What's your name?" Aaron asks as he motions for Nabin to translate. Though Aaron knows much of the local language, Nabin is originally from these villages and is also proficient in English, making communication much smoother and more accurate.

The man looks up. And as I look into his eyes, I can see into his skull.

"Kamal," he responds, covering the hole in his face with a cotton-like swab.

After a few minutes of small talk with Nabin translating, Aaron says to Kamal, "Can I ask what happened to your eye?"

Again looking down, Kamal answers, "A couple months ago, it became infected. At first, it itched and watered. I didn't think much about it, but then it got worse. I felt a sharp pain in my head. It didn't stop for many days. Finally, my eye fell out."

Aaron asks more questions, and Kamal shares how his cheek is caving in and his hearing is failing. As we listen, we realize what's happening. With no medicine available nearby, Kamal has an infection that is quickly overtaking his entire head, and may even end his life.

Aaron shifts the conversation in a more spiritual direction and asks, "Have you ever heard of Jesus?"

Kamal looks back, confused. "No, who's that? I've never heard that name." It's like Kamal is being asked about a man he's never met who lives in a nearby village.

Aaron begins to tell the story of Jesus, but Kamal seems confused about the relevance of a man who lived two thousand years ago. When Aaron finishes, Kamal just looks down and quietly says, "I need help for my eye."

Aaron has been part of starting a clinic farther down the mountain, and he tells Kamal he will work to get him some help.

"May I pray for you?" Aaron asks Kamal.

Though still obviously confused, Kamal answers yes.

Standing up to our knees in the snow, shivering from the cold, we gather around Kamal and pray for God to help him—in the name of Jesus.

## Praying in Faith

But even our prayers feel empty. At least to me. I know it shouldn't, because I know prayer matters. What could be more valuable than talking to God on Kamal's behalf? But that's just it—even as we say amen, I can't escape a lack of faith in my heart that the words we just said are going to make too much of a difference.

Praying sure felt like the right thing to do, but as we prayed, I wasn't really praying with actual faith that God would miraculously heal Kamal on the spot. And honestly, I'm not sure I had that much faith that things were ever going to change for Kamal. It's a pretty empty feeling to pray for someone when deep down inside you're not actually believing it's going to matter.

Surely that's not the way prayer is supposed to work. I teach all the time that this isn't the way prayer works. So why do I have these doubts in the hiddenness of my own mind and heart?

Discouraged at this moment by my empty-feeling faith, I'm encouraged by a totally different picture I see in Aaron. As we walk away, he tells us more about the clinic they have set up farther down the trail. There, Aaron says, Kamal will have the opportunity to get medical help while also hearing more about Jesus. In other words, I see in Aaron a picture of someone who believes what he just prayed—that we just spoke to the one true God, who has all the power in the universe to help Kamal. Aaron believes this so much that he is at God's disposal to be the means by which his prayers are answered.

I want to pray in faith like that—not just talk about praying that way.

## Urgent Needs

Leaving Kamal's village, the trail narrows significantly. No longer on a plateau, we now trek along a mountainside. It's startling to look to your left and see a steep drop into a deep canyon. If you slip now, it will be a long fall and you won't live to tell about it.

In these mountains, on a trail like this, it's impossible to walk next to another hiker. When walking single file, concentrating on your steps, meaningful conversation with anyone else is out of the question, so I find myself alone with my thoughts. As I reflect on what we just witnessed in the village, as well as on what Aaron said as we were leaving, I realize this was the perfect living definition of "urgent spiritual and physical need." Physically, Kamal is approaching death with seemingly no help in sight, and spiritually, up until twenty minutes ago, he had never even heard the name of the only one with the power to save him from sin and death.

I find myself thinking, *Are physical and spiritual needs equally urgent? What is Kamal's most urgent need?*

Surely you could make a case that Kamal's most pressing need is medical care. What he needs most right now is not a story about Jesus but help from a doctor. Yet someone else might say that hearing about Jesus is absolutely Kamal's most urgent need. After all, the mission of the church is to make disciples, not meet physical needs, right? In that moment on that trail, it seems to me that both needs are urgent and we can't ignore either of them. If we ignore both, then maybe we're the ones who are blind.

## Cholera Outbreak

After a time, the trail eventually widens as it winds away from the mountain ridge. This makes it easier for people to walk alongside one another. Or to pause and have a conversation with those who are coming up the trail.

That's exactly what happens when Aaron sees a man carrying his one-year-old son up the path. As soon as they see each other, they smile and greet one another with a hug. Aaron stops our team to introduce us: "This is Sijan, and his baby boy's name is Amir."

We have all picked up on the local greeting, so we say hello in the local language as we smile and slightly bow our heads.

"Sijan and Amir are from a village just up the path that way," Aaron says, pointing to a mountain ridge on our left. "Less than a year ago, right after Amir was born, their village experienced a cholera outbreak. I'm not sure how much you know about cholera, but it's a potentially deadly disease caused by eating food or drinking water contaminated by bacteria."

This reminds me that Aaron warned us early on to drink only tea that's hot—boiled—and otherwise drink only the filtered water from our water bottles.

"People who have ingested that diseased food or water experience watery diarrhea and severe dehydration," Aaron continues.

"Cholera is easy to treat if you have the right remedy. People can take an oral rehydration solution combined with antibacterial medicine and over 99 percent of them will recover just fine. If cholera is untreated, though, children or adults can die within a couple of days, and sometimes within a few hours."

Aaron pauses, looks knowingly at Sijan and Amir, takes a deep breath, and continues. "That's what happened in Sijan's village. Due to poor sanitation and unclean water, people became infected with cholera, and it spread like wildfire. They had no treatment, and within hours, people of all ages in the village were suffering. After only a couple of days, sixty were dead."

Our jaws drop. Can you imagine sixty people in your immediate neighborhood dying of diarrhea in two days, including several within your own family?

"Almost every home was affected," Aaron tells us. "Those sixty dead included two of Sijan's children—Amir's older brother and sister."

As if that weren't heavy enough, Aaron finishes the story. "In the aftermath of this outbreak, Sijan's wife—Amir's mom—was driven to depression and despair. She couldn't bear having lost two of her three children, in addition to so many friends and extended family. So one day Sijan's wife took a rope, found a tree, and hung herself."

As Aaron is telling this story to us in English, we look over at Sijan. He doesn't understand what's being said, so he's not paying close attention to Aaron. Instead, he's looking into his son's face as he holds him in his arms. A year before, he had a wife and three kids in his home. Now he's alone with his little boy.

"In the days after Sijan's wife died," Aaron says, "he passed Amir around to different women in the village who nursed him and kept him alive."

As I'm hearing this story and watching this father and son whose lives have forever been changed, I remember an article I read about seven hundred twenty-five thousand cases of cholera in Yemen in what the World Health Organization was calling "the worst cholera outbreak in the world."* Standing on this trail, I realize in a fresh way that all these cholera cases are not just numbers; they are people like Sijan and Amir. These are little boys and their dads, moms and their daughters, and grandparents who are dying of preventable diseases. How do we measure the urgency of that need?

Before leaving on this trip, one of my sons had made a bracelet for me to bring and give to a child I might meet. Obviously, I know a bracelet is not little Amir's greatest need, but I still long to give him and his dad something that will show them that some people from the other side of the world care about them. So I pull out the bracelet, and through Aaron translating to Sijan, I say, "My little boy made this bracelet for your little boy. I want to give it to you, and I want you to know that my family will be praying for you."

Sijan takes the bracelet, smiles, and slides it onto his son's wrist. As I watch Amir try to figure out what the bracelet is, Aaron and Sijan talk a little longer. Then we say goodbye and start walking again down the trail.

---

* "Yemen: Cholera Response," *Emergency Operations Center, Situation Report No. 5,* September 24, 2017, www.emro.who.int/images/stories/yemen/the_emergency_operatios _center_sitrep-5-English.pdf?ua=1.

Aaron is beside me and says, "As soon as we heard about that cholera outbreak, we rushed in some clean water filters. We also brought a water-sanitation system to Sijan's village and were able to get some specific health care for little Amir."

"That's fantastic, Aaron," I say. As we walk on, I'm thankful to be hiking with somebody who's doing something concrete about urgent need.

## Chained in a Barn

Along the trails, occasionally we stop to drink or fill our water bottles, more mindful now than before how critical clean water is. And we're spoiled, to say the least. Each of us has some sort of filtration system in our packs. Chris and Sigs each pull out a bag, fill it with water, and then screw a special filter on top of the bag. They then push the water out of the bag through the filter into their water bottles. My filter is actually built into my water bottle, so I simply scoop my bottle into a stream to fill it with water, put the top on, and drink directly from the filtered mouthpiece. Just like that, we are protected from all sorts of bacteria.

In Sijan's village, simple filters like this would have saved sixty people, including three members of his family.

By now we are trying to stay hydrated, and hiking up and down these high-altitude trails definitely is burning off any calories we gained by that small egg and bread we each ate a few hours before.

It's almost lunchtime, and we're all looking forward to some food and a break from the hike. Entering the next village, we find another teahouse, set our packs down outside, and squeeze inside for some warmth, water, and food.

Aaron orders tea, bread, and dal, a soup made of lentils and spices. As we sit around the table waiting for the food, Chris turns to Nabin, our translator, and asks, "Nabin, you were born and raised in these amazing mountains. Where are you from exactly, and what was it like growing up here?"

In the minutes that follow, what Chris thought would be a short, casual conversation as we wait for our meal turns into a long, sobering realization of what life really is like here. Nabin, although a tough-looking twenty-year-old, is humble and soft spoken. Speaking slowly and intentionally, he says, "I grew up not far from here. When I was very young, my mom died, and it was hard on my dad and me. My dad was very angry. Then one day my dad met another woman, and not long after, he decided to marry her. My stepmom had her own children, and she didn't like me. My dad started not to like me either and began beating me. He would take a hot switch from the fire and lash it across my back."

As Nabin continues, Aaron leans over and whispers, "Nabin still has marks all over his back from his dad."

This is surprising to me. I never could have imagined that Nabin had experienced such a childhood and that his well-worn shirt was hiding such scars underneath it.

"One day, I decided I couldn't take it anymore, and I ran away from my home into the mountains," Nabin says.

"How old were you when you did that?" I ask.

"About seven years old."

I'm stunned. I try to imagine one of my sons at age seven running away into the mountains, alone and afraid. More afraid of his dad—me—than of any danger in the mountains.

"I was fine for a few days, until my dad found me," Nabin continues, "and that was not a good day. He picked me up by my feet and starting banging my body against the rocks. Once he beat me, he brought me back home, but I wasn't allowed to live in the house anymore. Instead, my dad and stepmom chained me outside in the barn, and that's where I stayed."

"How long did you stay chained in the barn?" Chris asks.

"Until Aaron found me."

At this point in Nabin's story, our food arrives. Our host carefully places steaming-hot bowls of lentil soup before us. In the middle of the table she lays down a stack of roti, a circular-shaped flat bread popular in this part of the world. Aaron prays, thanking God for the food, and then we start to eat as Aaron continues the telling of Nabin's story.

"One day, I was hiking through this area, it was getting late, and I needed a place to stay, so I stopped in a village and went up to a random house. I asked if they had any room for me that night. They told me they didn't but that if I wanted to, I could stay in their barn. That was better than nothing, so I walked over to it, opened the door, stepped in, and closed the door behind me. I set down my pack, unrolled my sleeping bag, and laid it out on the floor. I took my shoes off and climbed in.

"But once I got in my sleeping bag," Aaron continues, "I heard a noise. I had assumed that the animals were in a separate area, but I thought immediately, *There's some kind of animal in here with me.* So I got out of my bag, turned on my flashlight, and started looking around that section of the barn. As my flashlight scanned, though, I didn't see an animal. Instead, I found the eyes of an eight-year-old boy staring back at me."

Chris and I exchange glances. This is unbelievable.

"Unfortunately," Aaron explains, "this is not that uncommon here. It's not unheard of for parents to keep their kids in the barn. Usually this occurs when a child has some kind of disability or deformity. Many villagers believe these kids are cursed, and they don't want the curse in their house. One handicapped child we found had been chained in a barn with the animals for ten years. So while I was startled by someone else in the barn with me, I wasn't shocked that it was a child."

"What did you do?" Sigs asks.

Nabin jumps back into the conversation. "He took care of me," he says. "He helped me find a home where I was cared for and I could go to school and I could learn about God's love for me."

We look at Aaron, whom we see is uncomfortable with the focus shifting to him.

"Let me tell you more about Nabin," he says. "Not too long ago, Nabin was hiking back up into the mountains and ran into his dad, who was coming down the trail with one of his stepchildren, who was sick. Nabin's dad asked if Nabin would go up the mountain and care for his wife, the stepmom, while he got help for this stepchild. In other words," Aaron says pointedly, "the dad who had beat and burned Nabin asked him to care for the mom who had wanted him chained outside their house in the barn."

"What do you think Nabin did?" Aaron asks.

We all are stunned by the story. No one seems to want to guess, so Aaron answers, "Nabin went up the mountain and stayed with his stepmom, personally caring for her over the next three months until his dad came back home."

Nabin, now really uncomfortable with the attention drawn to him, says to Aaron, "We should probably get back on the trail. We have a long way to go before dark."

We have finished lunch, so this seems a good time to move on. But I look at Nabin with new awe and respect. As he leads us outside the teahouse, I have a deeper perspective of what it's like to grow up in these mountains.

## Questions Without Answers

I don't get it. In the afternoon as we resume the trek, I fall behind the others on the trail and find myself alone in total confusion. I'm the preacher and pastor who's supposed to have answers, but at this moment I have nothing but questions without answers. This world, and my life in it, makes no sense to me.

I don't get why I was born into a family where my father loved and cared for me, while Nabin was born into a family where his father beat and burned him. I don't understand why since the first day I was born, I have had all the water, food, and vaccinations I have needed to protect me from preventable diseases, while today in the world, twenty thousand kids will die because they don't have those things available to them. I know there is a God, and I know he is in control of all things, but why have I received such blessing when so many others haven't?

It's certainly not because of anything I've done. I had nothing to do with where I was born. And neither did you, right? So why were we born into a setting where we have most everything we want, while millions, if not billions, of Sijans, Amirs, and Nabins don't have most everything they need?

Over the next couple of hours, I hike a few miles with my feet but I get nowhere in my head. *I just don't get it. Does God love me more than he loves men, women, and children in these villages? If so, why? If not, then what's the reason behind why I'm walking these trails with healthy legs instead of being born handicapped here and chained like an animal in a barn?*

Part of me wants to just stop and sit, think and pray, so I'm relieved when I catch up to the group at the next village. They're all sitting down with their packs at their sides, but as I walk up and Aaron starts to share, relief is not what I find.

## Missing Daughters

Aaron encourages me to drop my pack along with the others, grab some water, and find a rock to sit on while he shares something significant about this next village.

"The village we're about to walk into is a pretty good size. It's home to about two hundred people, but as you walk through it, I want you to notice something. Make note of the lack of girls in the village between the ages of about twelve and twenty. The reason is, most of the young girls here have been trafficked over the last five or so years, often starting when they are about seven but even up to fifteen years old. Specifically, they've been sold into slavery for sex."

Aaron goes on to explain how the trafficking industry works. "It's extremely well organized. Traffickers know the depth of poverty in these villages, and they will come through looking for homes of young girls in families who are struggling to survive. Such homes aren't hard to find.

"The traffickers pose as kind men looking to help these families. They promise parents that if they send a daughter down the mountain into the city with them, then they will help her get a good job where she can work not only to support herself but also to send money back up the mountain to support her family. Traffickers will promise to bring these girls back home periodically to visit and bring the money they've made. As a pledge of their promise, traffickers will give parents of a girl the equivalent of about one hundred dollars, a sizable sum [about half a year's income] for a desperate family in one of these villages. With these promises and this pledge, families then entrust their daughters to the care of these men."

"Don't families know after a while that the traffickers are lying—when the girls don't come back?" I ask. I am devastated by what I'm hearing.

"That's a good question," Aaron replies. "But poverty makes parents do desperate things. And they sincerely believe that their daughters are better off than being here."

All of us on the team look at each other and shake our heads. This is hard to believe.

Aaron continues. "After a tearful departure, these girls are then escorted down the mountains and smuggled past police check-points into the city. Some stay there in the capital, while others are transported to other cities and countries, never to return again.

"For the ones who stay in the capital, they are put to work in what is called a cabin restaurant. The booths in a cabin restaurant are like cubicles, with wood frames starting at the floor and reaching all the way to the ceiling. Those high wood frames conceal scenes of horror beyond what any of us wants to imagine."

*I almost wish Aaron would stop. This is so painful.*

"A man will come into a cabin restaurant, take one of these precious young girls by the hand, lead her into a booth, eat with her, drink with her, and have his way with her body however he pleases, either there in the booth or in a bedroom upstairs.

"And then another man will do the same thing.

"And then another man.

"And then another man.

"And then another man.

"Until sometimes fifteen to twenty men a day have had their way with one of these girls."

Aaron stops. Now we all are looking toward the village, deeply unsettled by what we've just heard.

I have an eight-year-old daughter. As I sit there on that rock, I can't even imagine this happening to her. I *won't* even imagine this happening to her. But that's a freedom I have that these girls don't have. This is their life. These girls who used to climb and play on these rocks on which I'm now sitting are gone, never to return to their families.

As we stand up and start walking through the village, we look around, and just as Aaron predicted, there are almost no girls in that age group. In what seems like a silent village, I find myself shouting inside, *Why, God? If you are in control of all things, then why do you let this happen? Why have you not saved these girls from this slavery? Why have you not struck down every single one of these traffickers?*

I don't understand. As we walk through and then out of this village, I don't understand why.

Nor do I understand *what*. I don't understand what this means for my life. Certainly it must mean something. Certainly I'm not supposed to see and hear these things and then go on with business as usual in my life. *But what do I do?*

That question sets the stage for one more encounter, which shakes me personally even more.

## The Face of Hunger

The one-hour hike after the last village is quiet. All of us string out on the trail, pondering what we've just heard and witnessed (or more accurately, didn't witness). Thoughts and emotions are spinning in my head and my heart. In the middle of it all, I feel an uncomfortable tension. On one hand, I just want these thoughts and emotions to go away. I want to be back home, where I don't have to think about a village pillaged by sex traffickers. This seems like too much reality. In a way, I want nothing more than to stick my head in the sand and pretend I never heard or saw what I've just experienced. It's like a bad dream, and I just want to wake up and realize that none of this is true.

On the other hand, I want to do something. *Now!* I want to find a trafficker walking down a mountain with a little girl, shut him down, and take her back home. Or I want to rush down these mountains and rescue as many of these girls as I can. But I don't know how. We've all heard that solutions to sex trafficking are complicated, and there are wise and unwise ways to go about fighting it.

Regardless of what it looks like, *I just want to do something.*

---

That tension I feel sets the stage for the final village we walk through today, a village that's much smaller than that last one. It's quaint and fairly quiet, and not many people are walking around. Most of the adults are likely still out working in fields on the mountainsides. I look to my left and see a row of about ten one- or two-room houses made of stacked wood. Outside each house is a pile of wood used for cooking and warmth. Snow covers everything in sight. Soon after we enter the village, two boys and a little girl, each of them about eight years old, run out from a house to greet us. The little girl's face is particularly encouraging to see in light of the young girls missing in the previous village.

Clearly, all three kids are impoverished and malnourished. Their faces are covered with dirt and their clothes are worn. Their smiles are bright, though, and the little girl grabs my hand to walk alongside me. As we stroll along, I think of my daughter, Mara, whom we adopted from a part of Asia not too far from here. Unable to speak this girl's language, I smile back at her as we playfully walk hand in hand.

I notice how thin she is and can guess she's hungry. I also remember what Aaron had told us before we left on the trek—how he had specifically advised us not to give out food. He and his team are intentionally addressing holistic needs in these villages, including access to clean water and sufficient food. So if one person starts handing out food to one child, then all sorts of other children would come running and want something—and their parents would come too. In the end, Aaron and his team have found that it's not beneficial long-term to provide short-term handouts to a few people here and there, creating more problems in the process.

But as we near the end of the village, my new friend—smiling sweetly and holding my hand—sticks out her other hand, as if asking me for something to eat. I have protein bars and trail mix in my bag, and I'm looking into the face of a little girl who needs that food far more than I do. I remember the instructions I was given and start to shake my head slightly, not wanting to say no, all the while trying to keep a smile on my face.

With a pleading look, she sticks her hand out again and says something I don't understand. I imagine it's something like, "Please, sir, give me something."

Again, I shake my head slightly, trying my best to smile.

That's when she raises her voice louder and tries to grab my bag. Reflexively, I turn my bag away so that she can't touch it. Not only am I not giving this hungry little girl some food, but now I'm physically, intentionally working to keep her from it.

In all of this, she's still holding on to my hand and we've come to the end of the village. The others on the team already have left, and I need to catch up, so I try to let go of her hand, but she won't let go of mine. She squeezes it—tighter. Now I'm not just keeping my bag from her, but I'm prying my hand away from this impoverished child who has walked with me, holding my hand, smiling at me all the way through her village.

Finally, I pull my hand away and the expression on her face quickly changes. She looks at me with desperate, angry eyes and suddenly tries to spit on me. But she doesn't have enough moisture in her mouth, so her saliva falls on her face. As she stares at me with her dark eyes, I look back at her with nothing to say. Everything in me wants to give her everything (or at least something!) in my bag, yet I turn and walk away. And I don't look back.

I walk, fast, but I don't know why. *What am I afraid of? What am I running from? And why do I feel like this?*

I preach sermons and write books on giving to the poor. I offer the same counsel that I received about not giving to the few so that the many are left out. I even wrote a foreword to a popular book on wise ways to help people in need without hurting them. Yet at this moment, none of what I've taught or written feels right, for on this trail I'm seeing in myself a tragic paralysis in the face of the poor. I'm so quick to say that I don't think this or that is the wisest way to help the poor and we shouldn't do or give to this or that project because of this or that reason. And certainly there's a place for evaluating the wisdom of what we do and how we give.

But at some point, don't we need to do *something* instead of running away and giving *nothing*? Surely I can't live my life always spouting excuses for why this or that doesn't work or isn't wise. Don't I need to spend my life figuring out what does work and doing it?

———

Hours later, in the teahouse where we will bunk overnight, I can't look at myself in the mirror. I can't look at the same face that a precious, hungry little girl—with saliva on her cheek—saw before I yanked my hand away and ran off with a bag full of food. In that mirror, I don't want to see a man who can so deftly talk about caring for the poor yet so quickly run away from doing so.

## An Eternal Perspective

Exhausted in every way, trying to stay warm in the freezing air, I huddle in my sleeping bag. With my headlamp I read verses from chapters 4–6 in Luke, beginning with this startling announcement from Jesus that it seems God has planned for me to read at this exact moment:

The Spirit of the Lord is on me,
because he has anointed me

to preach good news to the poor.
He has sent me
to proclaim release to the captives
and recovery of sight to the blind,
to set free the oppressed,
to proclaim the year of the Lord's favor. (4:18–19)

As I read, I journal,

*This is who Jesus came for! The people in these mountains! In one day, I've met the poor, the captive, the blind, and the oppressed. They're all here! And Jesus, you came to bring good news, freedom, sight, and love to all of them! So why are they missing all these things?*

*O God, I have so many "why" questions after today. And I don't know the answers. I also have "what" questions. What should I do in the face of such need? Surely running away is not the answer. Lord Jesus, I want your life in me to bring good news to the poor, liberty to the captives, recovery of sight to the blind, liberty to the oppressed, and your favor in the face of urgent physical need.*

While he was in one of the towns, a man was there who had leprosy all over him. He saw Jesus, fell facedown, and begged him: "Lord, if you are willing, you can make me clean."

Reaching out his hand, Jesus touched him, saying, "I am willing; be made clean," and immediately the leprosy left him. Then he ordered him to tell no one: "But go and show yourself to the priest, and offer what Moses commanded for your cleansing as a testimony to them."

But the news about him spread even more, and large crowds would come together to hear him and to be healed of their sicknesses. Yet he often withdrew to deserted places and prayed. (5:12–16)

*Talk about urgent physical need. Leprosy was not just an illness in this story; it was a deadly contagion. Those who had it were required to warn people around them not to get near them. Jewish law forbade touching lepers. So it's startling to see this man physically approaching Jesus. But what's even more shocking is Jesus's response. He doesn't just speak. He does what others would never do. Jesus touches him. Instead of running from him like everyone else, he reaches out to him like no one else.*

*O God, I don't want to run from those in need. I want to run toward those in need.*

*Please, O God, forgive me for all the ways I run from the needy instead of to the needy!*

But woe to you who are rich,
for you have received your comfort.
Woe to you who are now full,
for you will be hungry.
Woe to you who are now laughing,
for you will mourn and weep.
Woe to you
when all people speak well of you,
for this is the way their ancestors
used to treat the false prophets. (6:24–26)

*Jesus is promising a pretty massive reversal here. In eternity, many people will find themselves in an opposite condition from their situation on earth. That's a frightening prospect for the rich who ignore the poor. And I'm the rich.*

*So God, please help me not to ignore the poor. Please help me to live with an eternal perspective. Please help me to live with your love for the physically poor, hungry, and hurting.*

*O God, I pray for the poor I've met today. Please help them! And I pray that you would make my life a means by which those prayers are answered.*

## Reflections

What from this day's journey causes your heart to ache most?
What questions do you wrestle with most in the face of urgent
physical need?

Have you ever turned away from someone in urgent physical
need? Why did you turn away? If faced with a similar situation
again in the future, how might you respond differently?

# Day 3: Body Breakers and Butter Tea

## Compassionate Power

When you wake up early in the morning in a really warm sleeping bag and you know it's utterly freezing outside, you're content to lie there a little longer than normal.

So I pull out my Bible again, and before the day begins, I read,

> He was on his way to a town called Nain. His disciples and a large crowd were traveling with him. Just as he neared the gate of the town, a dead man was being carried out. He was his mother's only son, and she was a widow. A large crowd from the city was also with her. When the

Lord saw her, he had compassion on her and said, "Don't weep." Then he came up and touched the open coffin, and the pallbearers stopped. And he said, "Young man, I tell you, get up!"

The dead man sat up and began to speak, and Jesus gave him to his mother. Then fear came over everyone, and they glorified God, saying, "A great prophet has risen among us," and "God has visited his people." This report about him went throughout Judea and all the vicinity. (Luke 7:11–17)

*Here is a woman who had lost her husband, and now her only son has died as well. For a woman like this in the first century, she had no hope. She had no one left in her family to provide for her. So Jesus sees her and has compassion on her. Then, in his compassion, Jesus goes to the widow's son and raises him from the dead. Jesus transforms death into life.*

*Jesus, I praise you for your love for people and your authority over death.*

When Jesus returned, the crowd welcomed him, for they were all expecting him. Just then, a man named Jairus came. He was a leader of the synagogue. He fell down at Jesus's feet and pleaded with him to come to his house, because he had an only daughter about twelve years old, and she was dying.

While he was going, the crowds were nearly crushing him. (8:40–42)

*I imagine what it would be like if Jesus were physically walking through these valleys and villages right now and word got around that he had power to heal people of sickness. He would be surrounded at all times, just as he was two thousand years ago.*

A woman suffering from bleeding for twelve years, who had spent all she had on doctors and yet could not be healed by any, approached from behind and touched the end of his robe. Instantly her bleeding stopped.

"Who touched me?" Jesus asked.

When they all denied it, Peter said, "Master, the crowds are hemming you in and pressing against you."

"Someone did touch me," said Jesus. "I know that power has gone out from me." When the woman saw that she was discovered, she came trembling and fell down before him. In the presence of all the people, she declared the reason she had touched him and how she was instantly healed. "Daughter," he said to her, "your faith has saved you. Go in peace." (verses 43–48)

*Jesus, I praise you for your compassionate power on behalf of individual people. Everyone matters to you. I think of your love for every single person I'm meeting, or even seeing, in these mountains. O God, please help me to see every individual as you see him or her.*

While he was still speaking, someone came from the synagogue leader's house and said, "Your daughter is dead. Don't bother the teacher anymore."

When Jesus heard it, he answered him, "Don't be afraid. Only believe, and she will be saved." After he came to the house, he let no one enter with him except Peter, John, James, and the child's father and mother. Everyone was crying and mourning for her. But he said, "Stop crying, because she is not dead but asleep."

They laughed at him, because they knew she was dead. So he took her by the hand and called out, "Child, get up!" Her spirit returned, and she got up at once. Then he gave orders that she be given something to eat. Her parents were astounded, but he instructed them to tell no one what had happened. (verses 49–56)

*Jesus, you alone control death, and you alone can give life. There is no one like you. Yet so many in these villages (most, even) have never even heard of you. Why not? They need to hear about you! Please use us on this trip to introduce people to you.*

Lying in my sleeping bag with my journal in hand, I wonder how these pictures in God's Word might apply to our time on the trails today.

## Yaks on the Trail

I get up wearing the same clothes I wore the day before. All of us on the team agree that we're too cold to change clothes, and we figure that with only one change of clothes for the whole trek, we need to spend a few days in them anyway. So we roll up our sleeping bags and restuff our packs, then head to the teahouse, where we sit down for bread, omelets, and chai.

"We covered a lot of ground at a pretty good pace yesterday," Aaron says. "Today we'll slow down some because the lower we descend into an area called Taplejung, the more people we will see on the trails."

Rested and fed, we head out. Increased traffic on the trail is challenging, particularly in the narrow spots. As I shared earlier, walking along a mountain ledge is treacherous. It gets even more delicate when you meet another person. And it really is dicey when you meet a yak!

Let me fill you in on yaks. These dark-brown, solid beasts of burden with stocky legs resemble cows with huge shaggy coats for warmth in the extreme cold. Oh, and they have horns. Yaks are everywhere here and are immensely valuable animals to the villagers. Yak milk provides protein and nourishment not only through the drinking of it but also through its use in stews and butter. Yak dung is used as fertilizer in the fields and as fuel for stoves. Various parts of the yak can become food, and yak hair and hides are used for clothes and blankets. In addition, yaks are the primary source of transport for goods up and down the trails.

Herders strap all sorts of supplies onto the back of a yak and then put a bell around its neck. Then they will lead a herd of connected yaks up the trail. Yaks are surprisingly agile and sure footed, enabling them to walk up these steep and narrow trails with remarkable steadiness—and slowness.

This is where some yak anxiety emerges. We're walking along a narrow ledge next to the mountain, when ahead, still out of sight, we hear the sound of yak bells. We round that corner, and there in a line, we see about ten yaks walking right toward us. They're carrying supplies and not interested in negotiating this path with us.

You learn quickly that the best place to move when you see a yak coming your way is right up next to the mountain. I mean, embrace that mountainside! The last thing you want to do is give that mountainside position on the trail to the yak, because if you are left on the outside of the ledge and that yak decides to bump you, then you will tumble down the side of that mountain to your death, while the yak goes on with his day like nothing has happened.

So you hug the mountain as one by one these yaks tread slowly by you. Behind them is their herdsman, who is constantly prodding to keep his gang moving. Once they pass, you can resume your trek in peace, though you want to watch where you step. It's breathtaking (quite literally) how much dung these yaks will leave in their wake.

## Sky Burial

After a while, the trail widens and we come to a clearing. We walk for a while on a level plateau that eventually leads us near a large pile of rocks about twenty yards off the trail. We stop to take a closer look. The rocks are stacked in a circular mound that forms a sort of stage about as wide as a human body and as tall as I can reach with my hands. Thin wooden poles surround the rocks, and attached to the poles are white tattered flags, which are blowing in the wind as we approach. The site seems to have hosted a ceremony, so Aaron gathers us to explain what has gone on here.

"What's called a sky burial took place here," he says. "In Buddhist belief, once a person dies, their spirit is reincarnated in the body of another person or animal or object. Such reincarnation occurs in endless cycles of life and suffering until a spirit might potentially reach a state of nirvana. Consequently, when someone dies, their corpse no longer has any value. It is merely a shell meant to be discarded by those who remain."

Aaron pauses and moves a bit closer to the mound of rocks.

"So instead of burying the body in the mountains," he continues, "which is hard to do as a result of the rugged terrain, Buddhist monks will bring the body out to a burial site like this early in the morning. Family members and friends will also come, though they'll stay at a distance. The monks involved in the ceremony are called body breakers."

"I have a question," Sigs says. "Is every Buddhist who dies buried like this?"

"No," Aaron responds. "Not everybody does this, and it happens less often now than it might have happened years ago. But as is evidenced by this burial site, this happened here recently."

"So how does it work?" asks Sigs.

"Together, the monks use ritual knives to saw off limbs and slice the body into pieces," Aaron answers. "As each piece is cut, it's placed on top of the rock mound, where vultures then descend and eat. After the flesh and organs have been consumed by the birds, the body breakers use mallets to crush the bones. The purpose of the ceremony is to discard every part of the body so that none of it is left."

Honestly, this is hard information to digest. What he is describing sounds like something back home that might happen in a meat processing plant. Without Aaron's explanation, we could walk by this pile of rocks and the fluttering flags and have no idea of the ritual performed here.

Aaron definitely has our attention: "These physical actions are loaded with spiritual meaning for Buddhists living in these mountain valleys. Some believe a sky burial is a visible picture of a person's soul being offered to the spirits or gods in the mountains as that soul moves on to a new incarnation. Many believe it's a sign of compassion for creation to use a corpse to feed birds and provide nutrients to nature. All believe it's a picture of the emptiness of the body alongside an endless cycle of suffering for the soul."

As I listen and look at the site of this sky burial, my mind shifts toward what seems like a completely different focus than I had yesterday. A day ago, in village after village, I was confronted with urgent physical needs: A man with a missing eye. More than sixty people killed by cholera. A boy beaten, burned, and chained to a barn. Girls as young as seven years old sold as slaves for sex. A precious, angry little girl desperate for food. But the focus at the start of this day is not on physical need, as important as that is, but instead on spiritual need. It's overwhelming to stand in a place where just a few days before, the body of a man or woman or child was being carved, crushed, and offered to the birds. It's even more overwhelming to think about where that man or woman or child's spirit is now.

In other words, as important as that body's physical needs were, we're now getting an unforgettable reminder that a time comes when the body is no more. And what happens after that point in time really matters. It matters for that man, woman, or child. It matters for every single person in these mountains. It matters for me . . . and you.

And it doesn't just matter now.

It matters forever.

## Believing a Lie?

After Aaron finishes his discussion at the sky-burial site, along with everyone else, I walk away in silence.

We resume the trek, trudging along carefully and cautiously as I keep close to the mountainside on the trail, and again I am lost in my thoughts. I am struck by the obvious differences between biblical faith and Buddhist faith. I remember the first time I was really exposed to Buddhism, studying it at the state-sponsored university I attended during a time when I found myself questioning the validity of the biblical faith I'd grown up believing. My study of Buddhism, in addition to Islam, Hinduism, animism, and atheism, actually ended up strengthening my belief in the Bible and what it teaches about God, humanity, what is wrong in the world, and the hope we have for how it can change.

In the process of exploring various belief systems, I began to see the absurdity of universalism. I would hear people say that all religions or belief systems are fundamentally the same, with merely superficial differences. But the more I studied, the more I saw that this was nowhere close to reality. It's not just illogical but also ludicrous to say that an atheist who believes there is no god and a Christian who believes in God have the same fundamental belief. While it's completely valid for people to have different beliefs about God, both of their beliefs can't be completely true. God either exists or he doesn't, which makes one person's beliefs true and the other's false, regardless of how passionately one holds that belief.

Followers of Jesus believe that he is God in the flesh and died on the cross. In contrast, followers of Mohammad believe that a man cannot be God and that Jesus (though a "good man," according to Muslim belief) did not die on a cross.

These beliefs are essential to both of these faiths, yet they are extremely different. Either Jesus is God or he is not, and either he died on the cross or he did not. Again, it is entirely valid for over a billion people to believe one way and another billion to believe another way, yet the reality is that more than a billion people in this picture are believing a lie.

So here on these mountain trails, I am thinking more about Buddhism as I'm seeing the implications of Buddhist belief in practice around me. Those implications become even clearer as we enter the next village, where the team will split up to eat lunch in different homes.

## Mountain Hospitality

Aaron knows more people in this village, and he has asked different families to host us for bread and tea. So we set down our packs, split into two groups, and scatter around the village. One group is Aaron, Sigs, and Chris. Nabin and I head to a second home.

The two of us approach a one-room house. It's like a triplex, connected to other one-room houses on each side. The house has two stories: an area below that provides shelter for animals, and an area above that is a shelter for the family. The house is made of stone and wood, including rough, thick beams. We climb a ladder up to the second story and into the room where the family sleeps, eats, and does life in a quaint, small space.

As we climb into the living area, I find that the ceiling is low, so we crouch to not bang our heads. The room is inviting but dark and smelling of a hardwood fire mixed with incense. To our left we see a small open flame that's covered by a rectangular grate. On the grate sits a steaming cast-iron teapot. On one side of the room the family's sleeping mats are stacked against the wall. There's only one small window letting in dim light.

We exchange greetings—Nabin translates for me—and our hostess motions for us to come and sit by the fire, which is positioned against the wall, making three sides to sit, each with a small mat. Traditionally, in this culture, the oldest male in the home sits in the place of honor, which as you face the fire is on the right. Since the woman's husband is working now, she motions for me to sit in the place of honor. I feel awkward at first, but she insists. Our hostess busies herself making Nabin and me tea. We ask questions about her family and learn that she and her husband have a three-year-old daughter and a twelve-year-old son. Almost as if on cue, the three-year-old climbs the ladder and enters the room. As soon as she sees these strangers in her home, she shyly walks to her mom. She's absolutely adorable. We smile at her, and before long she's smiling back.

The mom then tells us about her twelve-year-old son. When he was five, the family sent him to the Buddhist monastery to become a monk. That's the practice for firstborn sons in this village. So the son lives there and sees his family only on special occasions.

As she makes the tea, she pulls out a thick, cylindrically shaped wooden tube approximately three feet long. She then scoops up a big glob of butter and dumps it into the bottom of the tube. Next she takes the steaming pot of water from the fire and pours some into the tube, where the butter waits. Then she pushes and pulls a long thick utensil up and down the tube to mix the water and butter together.

She repeats this process with another glob of butter, and another, and another, along with more and more hot water, until the buttery tea is ready to serve. She takes a cup the size of a coffee mug, pours the butter tea from the tube into the cup, and hands it to you. Once the liquid cools enough to drink, you begin sipping your tea. Sure enough, it tastes exactly like you would imagine a drink made with globs of butter and hot water!

The woman then offers us yak milk for the tea. Unsure of exactly how long the milk has been sitting out, I politely decline, telling her I'm yaktose intolerant. (Just kidding. I didn't really say that!)

As she starts to serve us bread, the husband comes up the ladder, so we quickly shift mats to make room for him at the place of honor. We introduce ourselves, which leads to conversation about his work and the family's routine. Sitting there, sipping butter tea from a cup in one hand and munching bread from the other, we begin to discuss what a normal day looks like for them.

They tell how they wake up around four or five o'clock in the morning and fix tea and bread for breakfast. Then the husband heads out to the field around sunrise. The wife goes out a bit later with her daughter on her back. He works there all day long until the sun begins to set around six o'clock, and she comes back earlier to prepare dinner. All of this, of course, is only when the weather allows. During the coldest months of the winter, the temperatures can dip below zero degrees Fahrenheit, so they stay inside all day and night. This is why they have to work all day when it's warmer—to cultivate and store crops and other needed supplies for the long, brutal winter.

As they're sharing, I see above the fire on a shelf a book next to what seems to be a Buddhist shrine, which is a small statue of the Buddha behind four candles in silver cups. "Could you tell me about your book and the statue?" I ask, pointing to the shelf.

Smiling, the father answers, "The book contains teachings about the Buddha. We can't read, so we wait for a monk to read teachings from the book to us. One day," he says proudly, "my son will be able to read them to us."

Then he tells us about the shrine. "Every morning when we wake up, the first thing we do is burn incense in front of the statue of the Buddha. We fill these silver cups with water and light the candles that are floating in them."

"Why do you do this every morning?" I ask.

"We want to have a good life in our next life," he explains.

"Better than this one," his wife says with what seems like a hopeful smile, glancing at her husband. He nods, then asks me, "You also do this, don't you?"

After an awkward pause, I answer, "No, I don't."

I begin to share with them a brief explanation of God and Jesus, at which point I ask, "Have you heard of Jesus?"

A confused look covers their faces. "No. Who is that?"

Just as Kamal responded to this question the day before, it feels like they're envisioning a man they've not met from another village. They have never heard about Jesus and have no idea who he is.

I start to tell them about Jesus, but immediately a variety of distractions divert their attention. Someone calls the husband outside and he excuses himself. His wife is pulled away by their daughter for a moment, and as soon as she comes back, she jumps back into trying to serve us more bread and tea. Nabin mentions that it's probably time for us to go, so I politely say no to her offer. Somehow she interprets my response as a yes, and she reaches for the tube to pour more butter tea into my cup. I lift up my hand saying, "I am good. I do not need more," which she interprets as the green light and tries to give me more. By this time, she's smiling and I'm laughing as we bob back and forth like a comedy routine.

That's when Nabin tells me, "If you put your hand over the cup, she'll know you're done."

So I cover my cup with my hand and say as best as I can, "Thank you." She smiles widely, as do I. That's all for the butter tea.

We rise to leave and thank our hostess profusely for her hospitality. Then we climb down out of the house and walk to our packs. As we go, we turn and look back, where we see the mom and her daughter smiling at us from the top of the ladder.

## How Will They Know?

As we leave this village, I dodge rocks on the path and think about the many similarities between this host couple and Heather and me. We both love our families, we're both proud of our kids, and we both work hard to provide for them (although I think their work in the fields is a lot harder than any work I've ever done). Moreover, we both have strong beliefs, and while those beliefs are extremely different, we both try to put those beliefs into practice from the moment the day begins.

But here's the big difference that I don't understand. Unlike Heather and me, why have this husband and wife and kids, and their ancestors before them, never even heard that there are other possible ways to believe and live? As they shared about their morning ritual before the Buddhist shrine, it was almost as if they assumed everyone in the world believes the same ideas and performs the same rites. As if everyone in the world believes in reincarnation and an endless cycle of life, suffering, and death—only to start all over again and again and again. As if everyone in the world knows that if we burn enough candles, then things will be better for us when we die.

But what if that's not true? Obviously, I would be accountable for the consequences if these Buddhist beliefs are true—if I choose to disbelieve them. But that's just it. *I've had a choice.*

This wife and husband, along with their son and daughter, apparently haven't had a choice. No one has ever told them that there might be another way to believe and live, so they live every single day performing their rituals, not realizing that if their beliefs are untrue, then their hope not only in this life but, more importantly, beyond this life is based on a lie.

As I continue on the trail, other questions rise in my mind. I certainly believe that Jesus is true. I believe that God so loves the world that he did indeed send Jesus, God in the flesh, to die on a cross as a payment for sin. I believe that Jesus rose from the dead in victory over sin so that everyone who believes in him will have eternal life. But while I believe this, I can't comprehend why two thousand years later so many people in the world still haven't even heard this. I read in the Bible how God doesn't want anyone to perish and how he wants everyone to trust his love. But how is it possible for them to trust his love if they never hear about his love?

People in these villages see the glory of God in the grandeur of towering mountain peaks every single day. Even as I'm asking myself these questions, I'm looking at majesty all around me. I really wish I could give you a picture in words of the scenes that relentlessly surround us on these trails. But it would be like going to the Grand Canyon, being handed a piece of paper, and writing down what you see. It's impossible to describe with words alone.

Suffice to say that as you trek these trails, creation all around you is shouting out the splendor of the Creator. Yet as beautiful as this landscape is, I realize in a deeper way that it's ultimately insufficient to communicate the depth of the Creator's love. For more than two thousand years, these spectacular mountains may have been declaring the glory of God, but not for one second have these majestic peaks ever said a thing about Jesus. God has revealed his greatness to every person in these villages, but hardly any of them have ever heard about his grace.

*Why is that?*

## Window into Hell

All my questions come to a head as we wind down the side of one mountain toward a river. Far below I see smoke rising from alongside the water but can't tell why. The closer we get, the more people we see congregating at the riverside. Clearly, something is taking place, but no one prepares us—or could have prepared us—for what we are about to witness.

As we near the river, we see a group of young men carrying what looks like a dead body wrapped in a white sheet. Stunned, we watch as they lay the body on a platform situated about twenty feet above the water. People are wailing around what we now recognize is a funeral pyre. After the body is placed on the pyre, an older man lights a torch and starts a fire at the body's feet, hands, and head. The white sheets turn dark, the dead body catches fire, yellow flames fly into the air, and black smoke mars the blue sky.

Aaron steps behind us and explains what's happening. He tells us this is a Hindu ritual. Hindus in this area believe this river is holy. So whenever a family member or friend dies, within twenty-four hours they bring the body to the river and set it ablaze. They believe that the body's ashes falling into the river helps the deceased in the process of reincarnation.

Others start to ask Aaron questions, but I just step away and sit down. I can't stop staring. As I look into these flames, I think about what I believe. About what I preach from the Bible—that all who do not trust in Jesus to save them from their sin will experience the payment for their sin in an eternal hell.

Hell, a place that Jesus himself describes as conscious torment. Outer darkness. And fiery agony. The Bible repeatedly describes hell as a lake of fire that people will never, ever leave.

Some people object, proposing that these biblical descriptions of hell are just symbolic. Maybe, some believe, the language isn't literal. But even if that's the case, we would need to ask the obvious follow-up question: What do we think these symbols of hell represent? A wintry retreat? A summer vacation? Clearly, these are not descriptions for a nice place. These are symbols for a terrifying place! The purpose of a symbol is to express a reality greater than what can be expressed in words, so it should bring no solace to think that the Bible's descriptions of hell might be symbolic.

So there I sit on the bank of the river, realizing that if what I believe is true, I am looking now at a physical picture of a spiritual reality. This person whose body is burning was alive twenty-four hours before and now is in hell, an eternal fire from which he or she will never be rescued.

Then, as if that realization is not heavy enough, it hits me. This person, like most every other person whose body is burned on one of these funeral pyres, not only is in hell, but he or she likely never even had a chance to hear about how to go to heaven. This person never heard how Jesus could save people from their sin.

Is this right? Is this reality? Do people who never even have a chance to hear about heaven on earth really go to hell for eternity?

I've preached on this hundreds of times, and I've written chapters in books on how the destiny of people who don't hear the gospel is eternal damnation. Yet in this moment, the weight of what I believe about "those people" feels a thousand pounds heavier as I look at "this person" whose body is now being devoured by the fire. At this time yesterday, this person was alive in one of these villages we're walking through. It's like I'm looking through a window into hell, and I'm struggling to believe what I'm seeing.

I am surrounded by the majesty of God in these mountains, but I am wondering where in this scene his mercy is to be found.

## Two Options

I look around and realize that I'm alone. I see the group headed up the trail on the other side of the river, so I quickly rise and run toward them. Apparently, Aaron was keeping an eye on me, and he lags behind until I catch up to him.

"Are you all right?" he asks.

"No," I admit, "I'm not."

"Tell me what you're thinking."

"I don't get it. I believe everything the Bible teaches about heaven and hell. I stand by everything I've preached and written about what happens to those who've never heard the gospel when they die. So why am I struggling to believe what I'm seeing?"

Aaron sympathizes. "I don't know anybody who believes in hell who doesn't struggle at some level with that belief. If there's no struggle with what you believe about hell, then you don't really believe in hell."

"Then why," I say as if it's the first time I've ever really asked the question, "if the gospel is true, are there so many people in the world who have never even heard about it?"

"That," Aaron says, "is the mystery to me."

We walk on for a while in silence; then he shares, "Here's the conclusion I've come to about hell. You and I and every person who comes into this place has two options for how we think and live based on what we see here."

"Okay, I'm listening."

"The first option is to disbelieve the Bible—to stare at burning bodies and decide that hell just isn't real. Or maybe just to decide that Jesus is not necessary to gain heaven. That people can go to heaven apart from faith in Jesus. But the only way to believe that is to disbelieve the Bible, so that's one option."

"And the second option?" I ask.

"The second option is to believe the Bible and to show that belief by spending your life sharing his truth and love in a world of urgent spiritual need. Not merely physical need," Aaron says, "as important as physical need is. But to live like people's spiritual need is their most urgent need."

I press him. "How can you say that? Yesterday we saw massive physical needs, and you're doing all kinds of things up here to meet those needs. Aren't they just as important?"

"No," Aaron answers. "Don't get me wrong—meeting those physical needs is extremely important. Getting water filters and medical kits and a sanitation system to that village devastated by cholera was an urgent need."

"Exactly," I start to say, but Aaron interrupts.

"But as helpful as those water filters are, the fact is, they won't get anybody in that village to heaven. And neither will the medical kits or the sanitation system. What that village needs more than anything else is the truth of God's love, which will give them life forever."

## The Most Important Need

Right after Aaron says this, someone ahead on the trail calls for him, so he hurries off to see what the person needs. That leaves me alone to process the events of the day as we approach the village where we'll spend the night.

As I contemplate the relationship between physical and spiritual needs, I'm reminded of a conference where I had preached a few months prior. About a thousand young Christian leaders from over a hundred countries were in attendance, and I was asked to speak for twenty minutes. I wasn't aware there was a social-media platform set up for the conference so that during each speaker's session, participants could dialogue with one another concerning what the speaker was saying. I didn't learn about this until after my twenty minutes were up, and then I discovered that what I'd said had created all kinds of debate.

Basically, I had talked about the very issues I was wrestling with today on the trail: the reality of an eternal hell and the priority of proclaiming the gospel to people who have never heard it. I'd shared how hell is real and lasts forever, just as the Bible teaches, which is why sharing the gospel is the primary work the church must do around the world.

After I finished, several of these young leaders had come to me wanting to debate whether or not hell was real or truly lasts forever. Others wanted to argue that mercy ministries and acts of social justice are just as important, if not more important in some situations, as sharing the gospel. Those conversations continued not only at the conference but in the following days and weeks after with the conference organizers, some of whom had similar concerns about what I had shared. In the end, I was perplexed as to why speaking about a biblical picture of hell and the importance of sharing the gospel was such a problem at a Christian conference.

Yet now, months later on this trek, as I walk and see what I see, I have a greater understanding of where these leaders are coming from. As I had seen up close and personal yesterday, the need is indeed urgent for social justice and mercy ministry amid massive physical need. Moreover, as I am seeing in a fresh way today, even the possibility (and even more so, the reality) of an eternal hell is devastating. And without question, there's much of me in this moment that wishes that hell were not true. I don't want that person whose dead body is still burning to be in hell forever and ever.

But that's when Aaron's words convict me to the core and I realize I have two options.

One, I can disbelieve the Bible. I can say that God's Word is not true. Or maybe more subtly, I can assert that God's ways are not right. I can convince myself that somehow I have more compassion than God himself, such that if I were in charge, I would never create a place called hell. In other words, I can quickly convince myself that I know better than God and his Word regarding what is right and good in the world.

The more I think about this option, the more I realize it is the essence of sin. Way back in Genesis, sin entered the world when the created ones thought they knew better than the Creator. Sin entered the world when man and woman convinced themselves they were right about what was good and God was wrong.

My other option is to believe God in his Word, the Bible, and show that belief by spending my life sharing the truth and love of Jesus in a world of urgent spiritual need. Without question, that includes working to meet urgent physical needs through mercy ministry aimed at social justice. But water filters, medical kits, sanitation systems, and scores of other resources, though critical for life on earth, won't get anyone to heaven. And temporary earthly suffering, however severe, pales in comparison to eternal suffering, which lasts forever.

## Hope Beyond Death

As I catch up with the group in the village where we're staying for the night, I remember the stories from Luke 7–8 that had started my day, the miracles of people raised from the dead.

Indeed, I realize this is the greatest need in every one of our lives, including every life in the Himalayas and throughout the earth: to have hope beyond physical death. All of us will die, because all of us have sinned. And that means all people need to hear and believe in the One who has loving authority over death.

After dinner with the team, as always we are ready for some warmth and bed. So as I settle in for the night, I pray and plead as I fall asleep,

O God, I choose to believe your Word. I don't claim to understand it, but I choose to believe it. I choose to believe that Jesus alone has power over death and authority to bring life. And, O God, I pray if this is true, then more than anything else, the people here need to know about Jesus! You know this! And I am realizing this in a way I never have before.

So I am pleading like I never have before! Please show your mercy in these mountains! Please show your mercy now, O God! Before another sky burial! Before more people are born, live, and die with all their hope in burning incense to a statue! Before more people are put on funeral pyres! It has been too long— far too long, O Lord—that the love and power and compassion and authority and name of Jesus have not been known here. Please, please, please show your salvation here! And please, O God, use my life however you want, spreading this gospel as the answer to every person in the world's most urgent need: eternal life with you.

## Reflections

Do you think spiritual need is more important than physical need? How does your answer to that question affect your daily life?

How do you process the reality that many people in the world have never even heard of Jesus? How do you think this reality should affect the way you live?

# Day 9: I Saw Tiny Lights Moving up the Mountain

## Before the Day Begins

We're sleeping in small rooms attached to teahouses along the trail. Each room has a bed: a raised wooden platform with a thin mat on top. There's a small space on the floor beside the bed to put a backpack. The walls are made with light wood paneling, as is the floor, which creaks with every step. It's impossible to get up and head to the restroom in the middle of the night without making a good bit of noise. But you want to avoid that journey at all costs, anyway, because once you zip up in that sleeping bag, you don't want to go anywhere. Remember, you're sleeping in subfreezing temperatures.

When you walk into your room at night, it's pitch black and you have your headlamp strapped on in order to see, as there's no electricity. You survey the small room as best as you can, making sure to check for any creatures that could be joining you for the night. Himalayan jumping spiders are the highest-known permanent residents on the earth, living at heights of up to twenty-two thousand feet in the mountains. They are apparently pretty fascinating creatures, but I have no desire to share a residence with one of them.

Seeing no creatures (hopefully!), you set down your pack and pull out your sleeping bag. You lay it across the mat and then do anything else you need to do to prepare for bed. Once you're ready, you take off your shoes and jacket and jump in as fast as you can. You immediately zip up the side of the sleeping bag all the way until it covers your head and face, leaving only a small gap for you to breathe through.

Then it sets in. The heat trapped in that sleeping bag triggers a warmth you've not felt all day. And after all those miles hiked on the trails, it doesn't take long for that heat to lull you to sleep. Ideally, that sleep is uninterrupted until the rising sun peeks through the cracks in the wooden panels and it's time to start again.

That sun wakes me up today, and I'm not in a hurry to climb back out into the cold. So I unzip my sleeping bag barely enough to be able to read my Bible and jot down a few thoughts. This morning I'm in Luke 10, where I read, among other things, the following story:

> An expert in the law stood up to test him, saying, "Teacher, what must I do to inherit eternal life?"
>
> "What is written in the law?" he asked him. "How do you read it?"
>
> He answered, "Love the Lord your God with all your heart, with all your soul, with all your strength, and with all your mind," and "your neighbor as yourself."
>
> "You've answered correctly," he told him. "Do this and you will live."
>
> But wanting to justify himself, he asked Jesus, "And who is my neighbor?"
>
> Jesus took up the question and said: "A man was going down from Jerusalem to Jericho and fell into the hands of robbers. They stripped him, beat him up, and fled, leaving him half dead. A priest happened to be going down that road. When he saw him, he passed by on the other side. In the same way, a Levite, when he arrived at the place and saw him, passed by on the other side. But a Samaritan on his journey came up to him, and when he saw the man, he had compassion. He went over to him and bandaged his wounds, pouring on olive oil and wine.

Then he put him on his own animal, brought him to an inn, and took care of him. The next day he took out two denarii, gave them to the innkeeper, and said, 'Take care of him. When I come back I'll reimburse you for whatever extra you spend.'

"Which of these three do you think proved to be a neighbor to the man who fell into the hands of the robbers?"

"The one who showed mercy to him," he said.

Then Jesus told him, "Go and do the same."

(verses 25–37)

As I reflect on this reading, I take a minute to journal,

*I love you, God. I lie here in this sleeping bag before the beginning of this day in total awe of you and your love for me. I don't understand the mystery of your love for me, but I thank you for it. I want to love you with all my heart and soul and mind and strength, and I want to love others as you have called me to. Please teach me what that means.*

By this time, I can hear everyone else up and moving around, a cacophony of creaking! I know breakfast will be served fairly soon, so I climb out of bed and save reading Luke 11 for later. Along with everyone else, I roll up my sleeping bag and stuff everything into my pack, then walk up to the teahouse for tea, bread, and an omelet.

It's snowing this morning, and we sit around the breakfast table wearing our jackets, gloves, and hats. You can tell that we really enjoyed that warm night's sleep and weren't quite ready to get up and reimmerse ourselves in the cold. As we make shivering, groggy small talk, we see each other's breath as white puffs in the air. Whenever someone pours masala tea into a cup, the steam from the thermos rises like smoke. We each have both hands on the warm cup as we sip the tea and eat.

As breakfast wraps up, Aaron explains what to expect on this day.

"The hike today is going to be long, up through a region called Gasa, and we won't be able to stop somewhere for lunch. Be sure to drink plenty of water and keep some snacks or bars handy to eat along the way."

Each of us shuffles through the backpack for the items he suggested.

"Oh, and be really careful where you step today," Aaron warns. "Some of the trails will be narrow and quite steep."

With that, he tells us it's time to go. We shoulder our packs and step out onto the snow-covered trail.

## A Heart Problem

Not long after we start, because of the narrowness of the trail, we're unable to walk alongside each other and talk. We hadn't been very talkative this morning anyway, so we seem fine to have some time alone with our thoughts. Besides, the snow makes the trail slippery, so we are concentrating more on every step.

As I walk, my mind goes back to what I read in Luke 10. That expert in the Jewish law asked a really good question: "What must I do to inherit eternal life?" (verse 25). As I think about all I've seen on this trip, I realize that this really is the most important question of all. From preventable diseases to cholera outbreaks, from sky burials to funeral pyres, I can't think of a more important question for my life and the life of every single person in these mountains. In the world, really.

I think of how easy it is to be distracted by far more trivial questions. *What's the latest news? What are the current fads? Who's saying what on Facebook, Twitter, or Instagram? How's my 401(k) doing? How's my favorite sports team going to do this year?* My experiences so far have a way of putting those questions in perspective.

Jesus answers the lawyer's question with a question. I hate it when someone does that to me! Yet Jesus is the master of it, particularly with religious leaders, and he always does it for a reason. The man responds correctly, basically quoting what Jesus has said are the first- and second-greatest commandments: love God and love others. So Jesus affirms him. According to Jesus, eternal life is found in loving God with all your heart and loving your neighbor as yourself.

As I reflected in my journal, I want to love God with all my heart, and I'm overwhelmed by his love for me. But what about that second phrase? "Love your neighbor as yourself." Again, I think about all that I've seen the last couple of days, and I wonder what this really means. What does that kind of love look like here? What would it look like for me to love these people as myself? It hits me that if I were actually doing this, it doesn't seem as though I would be hiking like I am right now.

If I loved Kamal as I love myself, it seems like I'd be personally escorting him down the mountain to the clinic to help him get treatment for his eye.

If my eight-year-old daughter had been trafficked for sex, I'd be doing everything in my power right now to get down that mountain and find her. So if I loved these families as I do myself, then why am I not running down that mountain to help them find their daughters?

If I loved that hungry little girl in that village as I love myself, it sure seems like I'd have given her all the food I have in my bag.

If I loved that family who hosted me in their home for butter tea as I love myself, I'd still be there, talking with them about the love of Jesus that makes eternal life possible, not based on lighting candles and burning incense but based on trusting in what Jesus did on the cross for all people.

If I loved those people who were mourning around funeral pyres as I love myself, I'd have stayed at that site and spent every waking moment telling mourners how Jesus has conquered death and made eternal life possible for them. I'd have asked them who they knew were on their deathbeds in any village nearby so I could go and share that good news with them before their bodies were placed on those pyres.

How in scenes like this do I love my neighbor as myself? In

a world like this, how do we possibly love our neighbors as ourselves?

But even as I start to ask those questions, I sense myself starting to justify why I've not done any of the above things. I start coming up with reasons why taking this or that action wouldn't be wise for this or that reason. And suddenly, amid my search for self-justification, I realize that I'm a lot like the lawyer in this story. In Luke 10:29, I see a mirror of my own heart in a man who "wanting to justify himself . . . asked Jesus, 'And who is my neighbor?'"

This man wants clarification about who his neighbor is so he can know if he's doing enough to have eternal life. And that's the key to the story Jesus then tells.

The road from Jerusalem to Jericho is a steep seventeen-mile downhill road filled with all kinds of caves, rocks, and crevasses along the way. As I think about it, it's not all that different from the hike I'm on now (although I wish I were walking only downhill instead of uphill on these steep climbs here and there). Apparently, it was common for criminals to hide out in those caves, and in Jesus's parable, a man gets attacked by some robbers. They strip him of his clothes, beat him to a pulp, and leave him for dead.

Not long thereafter, a priest comes by, and he knows that God's law says if you meet a stranger in need, you do whatever it takes to meet his need (Leviticus 19:34). As I'm imagining this story play out, I think, *This is exactly who this man needs to walk by at this point.* But Jesus says the priest sees him and passes by on the other side. Literally, the language in the story depicts the priest looking at the man, then running in the opposite direction. *Kind of like I did a couple of days ago.*

Thankfully, though, the man has a second chance for help in a Levite, basically like a priest's assistant. But just like with the priest, Jesus uses the same language to describe how the Levite turned and went the opposite way around the man. So the irony is clear: the two leaders among the people of God who are charged with helping the needy are actually ignoring the needy. The tension in the story is thick. Who will love this man who is dying?

That's when Jesus inserts the shocking twist. "But a Samaritan," Jesus says. A hated outsider. A half-breed whom Jewish people believed polluted the line of God's people. When Jewish leaders wanted to discredit and offend Jesus, they called him a Samaritan. So as soon as Jesus mentions this word, you can sense the lawyer's blood start to boil.

The story continues as the Samaritan stops, assesses the man's need, washes the man's wounds, and takes him to the nearest inn, where he foots the entire bill for the man's complete care. And by the end of the story, Jesus has totally transformed the question. The question is no longer "Whom do I need to love?" Instead, the question is now "Who is the one who is loving?"

In response, the lawyer can't even bring himself to say *Samaritan,* so he simply says, "The one who showed mercy to him." Jesus tells him, "Go and do the same" (Luke 10:37). And in the course of one short story, Jesus stuns this man from the religious elite into realizing that what the law means when it talks about love is something far deeper than religious knowledge and religious responsibility. The kind of love God's law elicits is much greater, much riskier, much costlier, and much more uncomfortable than the lawyer had ever imagined.

As I traipse through the falling snow on that narrow trail, I realize in a fresh way the wonder of what this story means. It's not just a story about helping people in need without prejudice. If that were the case, Jesus could have easily described a Jewish man like the lawyer coming down the road and seeing a Samaritan in need. And even though the Jewish man had all kinds of prejudice, he stopped and cared for the Samaritan anyway. Then the meaning of the story would be clear: care for people in need, regardless of your prejudice.

But that's not the story Jesus tells. Instead, Jesus deliberately takes the lawyer on a winding narrative that shows the failure of the religious elite (that is, the priest and the Levite) to live up to the law of God. Then he brings a Samaritan into the story to expose the deep-seated hatred and prejudice in the lawyer's heart toward Samaritan people. In the process, Jesus makes the point clear: this lawyer needs a new heart. Just like we all do. There is a kind of love for God and for others that simply can't be manufactured by religious learning.

It makes sense as I think about it. I just imagine how the lawyer's conversation with Jesus could have gone a totally different direction from the start. Remember, he said that the law says love God with all your heart and love your neighbor as yourself. And Jesus responded, "Do this and you will live." But what if the man, at that point, didn't desire "to justify himself" by asking "Who is my neighbor?" What if, instead, the man desired "to humble himself" by saying, "Jesus, I can't do that. I can't love God perfectly, and I can't love others unselfishly. I need help to love like this." The conversation from that point would have been totally different, right?

And that's where I find myself now. Through the scenes around me and now this story before me, I find myself face to face with a lack of unselfish love in my heart. In all my religious learning and responsibility, I find it dangerously easy to walk past urgent need and do nothing about it. And I need God to change that in me.

## Tears into Tactics

*So what do I do?* I wonder. Right about that time in the trek, we come to a clearing and I see Aaron up ahead. I pick up my pace to catch up with him and say, "Can I ask you a question?"

"Sure," he responds.

So I dive right in. "On the first day of this trek, in the first teahouse we visited, right after we got off the helicopter, you told us you first came to this region twenty years ago with your college friends. You said you were planning to hike for weeks but at your stop that first night, you encountered something that kept you from sleeping. You said you cried all night long, and then you packed your bags and went back down the mountain."

He nods, so I ask, "What was it you encountered? What made you head back down the mountain?"

Aaron smiles briefly; then his expression turns serious. "I met a trafficker," he says. After a long pause, he continues. "My friends and I were eating dinner at this rest stop, and we were talking with a man we could tell spent a lot of time up here. And he started bragging to us about all the girls he had met up here. He told us how he would take the girls out of their impoverished conditions down into the city for work. He described how the girls make a living while men like him get pleasure."

Tears swell in Aaron's eyes as he continues, his voice now trembling. "The way this man talked about these girls was maddening. He viewed them as nothing more than objects to be used and abused however he and others wanted.

"Just as soon as the man finished talking," Aaron continues, "he said he needed to go, and he got up from the table and left. As I watched him walk away, I just sat there in shock. For a few moments, the guys around me talked about how horrible what this man said was, but before long they were talking about how eager they were to get to bed and get started hiking again the next morning."

Aaron pauses again—he's obviously reliving the moment and is moved. "But I couldn't get my mind off what that man said. I was totally numb. I couldn't believe what I'd just heard. And I couldn't stop thinking about it. I couldn't stop thinking about those little girls."

Tears now fall down Aaron's face as he says, "I went to bed that night, and I just lay there crying, all night long. Then I got up the next morning, and I knew I couldn't continue on like nothing had just happened. I told my buddies to go on without me. I hiked down the trail by myself, and for the last twenty years, I've been working to turn those tears into tactics for making God's grace known among these people."

As we walk next to each other, I have no idea what to say in response to Aaron's story. Aaron can tell I'm wrestling through a lot and says, "Your question is a good one, but just a little bit off. You asked me what made me head back down the mountain that morning, but the answer is not 'what.' The answer is 'who.' David, God did a work in my heart that night that caused me to come back down that mountain. God created in me a love for these people and a longing to show his love to them in any way I can with my life. That's the reason I'm here right now."

About that time, the path narrows again and Aaron moves in front of me. "We're about to head up a steep trail on the side of this mountain," he says. "Take your time and watch your steps."

As we start the incline, the irony is not lost on me. Listening to Aaron's story in light of Jesus's story in Luke 10, I realize that God is calling me to new heights of love for him and others. To a kind of love that goes beyond all my religious learning or sense of religious responsibility. To a kind of love only God can create. A kind of love that causes you to change the plans you might have had for your life or your family or your future. A kind of costly, uncomfortable love that's neither complacent nor content to protect yourself from the needs of those around you.

As I climb carefully up the trail, I think, *I long for this kind of love to mark my life.*

## False Summits

Aaron is right about the trail. It's straight uphill, and before long my thighs and calves feel like they're on fire. The stress on muscles is compounded by the stress on lungs. When people told me about training for this trek, some suggested hiking with a surgical mask on in order to simulate the challenges of breathing at higher altitudes with reduced oxygen. Others suggested hiking while breathing only through a straw. Both of these training methods sounded kind of weird to me, so I'd ignored both suggestions.

What that means is that on this particular trail, I (along with others who'd not prepared that much) now find myself walking about ten steps up the mountain and then pausing to enjoy the scenery (that is, catch my breath). Needless to say, hiking more than fifteen hundred feet up the side of a mountain ten steps at a time affords plenty of opportunity to enjoy the scenery.

This trail is not only steep; it's deceptive. As I look ahead, I see what appears to be the crest of the mountain. It seems far away, but I convince myself it's doable. So slowly, methodically, I start making my way up, ten steps at a time. The last sets of ten are the hardest, but I press on, knowing that I'm almost there. I find the will to endure because I know I'm almost at the end. Only twenty more steps to go. Then only ten steps. Until I finally finish that last step, ready to rest at the top of the mountain, only to realize that I haven't made it to the top. In fact, I'm nowhere close. A false summit! This mountain rises far higher than I'd imagined, and I'm only about a quarter of the way up its side.

This is a low moment on the hike, and when it happens, we all decide we need a mental game plan for making it the rest of the way. Personally, I can see the top of the mountain (or at least what I think looks like the top!), and I decide I'm going to split the trek into halves. I'll go as hard as I can for the first half, and then I'll take a long break. Then I'll split the rest of the trek into half again, taking a short break before ascending to the top. Convinced my plan will work, I drink some water and start climbing.

The first half is indeed hard, taking well over an hour, and with only intermittent pauses that entire time, I'm ready for a break. Alone about halfway to the top, I stop and find a flat rock on which to have a seat. I pull out some snacks and my water bottle. At eye level I'm surrounded by splendor on all sides.

## Shameless Boldness

Could there be a more magnificent place on earth than this to spend time alone with God? When the Bible pictures Jesus going aside on a mountain to pray alone, I now think of this scene. Out of breath and with wobbly legs, I'm not in a hurry to go anywhere at this point, so I decide to pull out my Bible and journal. I read the first part of Luke 11:

> He was praying in a certain place, and when he finished,
> one of his disciples said to him, "Lord, teach us to pray,
> just as John also taught his disciples."
> He said to them, "Whenever you pray, say,

Father,

your name be honored as holy.

Your kingdom come.

Give us each day our daily bread.

And forgive us our sins,

for we ourselves also forgive everyone

in debt to us.

And do not bring us into temptation."

He also said to them: "Suppose one of you has a friend and goes to him at midnight and says to him, 'Friend, lend me three loaves of bread, because a friend of mine on a journey has come to me, and I don't have anything to offer him.' Then he will answer from inside and say, 'Don't bother me! The door is already locked, and my children and I have gone to bed. I can't get up to give you anything.' I tell you, even though he won't get up and give him anything because he is his friend, yet because of his friend's shameless boldness, he will get up and give him as much as he needs.

"So I say to you, ask, and it will be given to you. Seek, and you will find. Knock, and the door will be opened to you. For everyone who asks receives, and the one who seeks finds, and to the one who knocks, the door will be opened. What father among you, if his son asks for a fish, will give him a snake instead of a fish? Or if he asks for an egg, will give him a scorpion? If you then, who are evil, know how to give good gifts to your children, how much more will the heavenly Father give the Holy Spirit to those who ask him?" (verses 1–13)

Sitting here gazing at several peaks more than fifteen thousand feet in the air around me, I reflect on this passage, specifically the story in the middle, with newfound awe.

The setting is first-century Palestine, where people bake enough bread for each day's needs and then start again the next day. So a guy shows up at his buddy's house and he's hungry. Unfortunately, though, the buddy doesn't have any bread. Hospitality is hugely important, so the buddy has a dilemma. On one hand, he can be a poor host and not give his friend any bread. Or on the other hand, he can go and try to find some bread from someone else at midnight. So he can either be a poor host or a poor neighbor. After thinking about it, the guy decides to take what's behind door number two.

His neighbor and his neighbor's family are already fast asleep. Houses in that setting had one room, which meant everybody slept together. I can imagine getting kid one, kid two, kid three, and kid four down for bed, then mom and dad lying down next to them quietly, knowing the slightest sound could wake up all of them at once, including the toddler it's taken an hour to get to sleep in the first place.

So while this nice man is fast asleep with his family inside the house, a knock comes at the door, and the guy on the outside says, "Friend." That's a good way to start when you're waking up someone at midnight, because this "friendship" is pretty fragile at this point. I can imagine that dad waking up and looking over at the two-year-old, whose eyes are now popping open. This is irritating! So that dad says in the politest way possible, "Don't bother me. I'm not getting up and giving you anything."

Then Jesus says that even though the dad doesn't want to get up because the guy outside is his friend (which is now in question!), he will get up because his buddy is shamelessly bold—basically a pest!

Now, the interesting thing about parables is that we read them and think, *Okay, somebody in this parable is me, and somebody in this parable is God.* So the disciples are thinking, *You and I are like the guy knocking on the outside of the door, but who's God here? Is he the grumpy guy on the inside of the house yelling "Don't bother me!"?*

Just what is Luke 11 teaching us about prayer? If you want something from God, just keep banging on the door and asking him for something. Eventually, he'll get annoyed enough to get up and do something for you not because he loves you but because you've bothered him to death. So now let's pray?

I don't think that's the point of the story. I think we find the message in his boldness. Jesus couches this story in the context of a question. He imagines a man who is so bold that he will go to his friend at midnight just for a piece of bread. Jesus is painting a picture of a shameless guy who doesn't know which social lines to cross or not cross. Do you know people like that? Or are you one? (You probably don't know it if you are!) This guy in the story doesn't get that you don't wake up your buddy and his entire family at midnight unless you have a really good reason. But he's so bold, so shameless, so pesky that he thinks, *I know my neighbor has what my friend needs, so I'm going to ask him for it,* and that, Jesus says, is how we should pray.

As I sit there on the mountainside reading this story, the wonder of prayer hits me in a whole new way. Here I am, looking out at God's glory on display in creation around me, and I realize it does seem bold for me, one person among more than seven billion people on the planet, to come to the one true God over all and Creator of all and say, "I know you have a lot on your plate running a universe right now, but I need you to listen to me. I have some things to ask you for, and I need your attention."

Doesn't that seem bold? Shameless? Brazen? Yet in this parable, Jesus is saying, "Be as bold, shameless, and brazen as you want."

Indeed, God has invited me, and you, to come to him anytime with anything, particularly (according to this story) on behalf of people who are in need. And so there on the side of that mountain, I pull out my journal and start writing out what feel like bold, shameless prayers.

*O God, you see the needs in these villages. You see the needs in these people's lives. You see Kamal's face caving in. You see Sijan and Amir in their suffering. You see Nabin's pain. You see these little girls being trafficked. You know where every one of them is right now and what they're having to do for evil men at this moment. You see that little girl who tried to spit in my face. You see those monks performing sky burials on dead bodies. You see people dying and being taken to the river, where they're set on fire. You see what's happening as they go to hell! O God, you see all these things!*

*So I'm knocking on the door right now, and I'm pleading, O God, I'm pleading for your mercy for them. Please, O God, show your healing power. Please, O God, give sustenance amid suffering and peace amid pain! Please, O God, save these little girls, and either save or smite those who sell and enslave them! Please, O God, provide for the poor, and please save people from eternal suffering! O God, you have the ability and authority to do all these things, and I'm asking you—pleading for you—to answer!*

As I pray and plead halfway up the height of my trek on that mountain, I fall on my knees and find myself experiencing new depths of boldness in prayer before God. I hope it's humble, and I believe it's heartfelt—more heartfelt than I've prayed in a long time. I believe what I'm praying, and I believe that the God who formed these valleys and mountains is listening.

Picking up my journal again, I write,

*O God, please glorify yourself in these mountains. Please cause your name to be hallowed in all these villages and all these valleys.*

*This is how you have told me to pray, and so I pray, and I plead for you to answer this prayer for your name's sake! Please cause your name to be known as great and gracious and glorious here! Please cause your kingdom to come and your justice and mercy and righteousness to reign here as they do in heaven!*

## Tiny Lights

From my knees, I'm startled as I turn around and see that Sigs has joined me on this flat spot. He's breathing hard but has a smile on his face. "This is a good place to stop," I tell him as I get up, reflecting on the time I've just spent with God. "You can get some great pictures here as well. I'll let you have this rock." I pick up my pack and slide it on my back and say, "I'll see you at the top."

"For sure," he answers, still catching his breath and grabbing his water bottle. "Maybe I'll even pass you—I won't be here long."

"Yeah, right," I answer. We both smile, because he knows how competitive I am—with a head start, there's no way I'll let him catch me!

I step out on the last half of the hike up the mountain. Buoyed by rest, I find new momentum on the trail. I can now average about twenty steps per intermittent pause, and it ends up taking about another hour to finally reach the crest. Aaron is waiting (he's been there a while), and he's already found a teahouse in a village that overlooks several valleys.

"This is where we'll stay for the night," he says, "and the timing is perfect."

"What do you mean?"

"The only church that exists in these villages is meeting here tonight, and it looks like we're going to be able to worship with them. Would you mind encouraging them with a message from the Word?"

"I would love to!"

"Great. For now, go ahead and put your pack down in a room," Aaron says. "Then rest for a bit. We'll have dinner in about an hour. Later, once it's dark, the church will meet just across the way."

I can't wait! We haven't encountered anyone who has even heard about Jesus for several days, so I'm eager to gather with people who not only have heard about him but also know him.

I find a room, set my stuff down, pull out my sleeping bag, and climb into it for a little warmth. I open my Bible to finish Luke 11 and then think about what to share that evening. But I fall asleep, and the next thing I know, Chris is punching my bag. "Get up, dude! It's dinnertime."

We gather in the teahouse for some bread and lentil soup. After we eat, Aaron invites us outside. It's pitch dark now and the sight of the stars is amazing. But Aaron hasn't brought us out here to look at the lights above. He points to a valley where we can see a few tiny lights that are moving up the mountain toward us.

"Do you see those lights?" he asks. We nod and he tells us, "Those are church members. Remember that grueling hike you climbed today to get up here? That's the hike they're making to get to church."

Humbled, I see these tiny lights in the distance slowly making their way up the trail. I think about the stress people in our culture sometimes have over a fifteen-minute-or-longer drive to church. How about a two-hour hike up a narrow mountainside in the freezing cold, followed by a two-hour hike back down the same mountainside in the pitch-black darkness after the service?

## This Is It!

The church meets in a house about a five-minute walk from where we're staying. This definitely is a "house church." Picture an area in a home in the US that's about the size of a bedroom or possibly a small living room. There's a bed in the corner (again, envision a raised wooden platform with a thin mat on top of it), a couple of shelves against the walls, and a small cooking area in the corner. One light bulb hangs suspended in the middle of the room.

When we arrive, the owner of the house greets us with a warm smile. She motions for us to sit in seats of honor, either on or right next to the bed. Soon others arrive, and we're shocked to see who has climbed that mountain to come to church. It's not just the young and healthy. Every age is present, from babies to grandparents.

One by one they start to cram in, and *cram* is the right word. By the time everyone arrives, I count more than fifty people sitting on the floor, on the bed, or on top of each other. They will sit in the most uncomfortable positions with smiles on their faces for the next two hours. They will sing, clap, pray, and listen intently as I share from Scripture.

When I'd prayed earlier about how to encourage this church, I thought about its makeup: men and women who live in a very difficult environment, physically poor, in a battle every day for the most basic needs of food, water, and medicine, and persecuted for their faith.

Before the meeting, the church's pastor had shared with me that his non-Christian parents died when he was just fifteen. A few years later, someone shared the gospel with him for the first time. He trusted in Jesus and was baptized, but as soon as this happened, the rest of his family abandoned him. His brothers told him to never come back, and he lost the inheritance his parents had left him.

But this pastor and his people believe that Jesus is worth it. "Jesus is worth losing your family," the pastor told me. Then he quoted Mark 10:29–30, saying,

> "Truly I tell you," Jesus said, "there is no one who has left house or brothers or sisters or mother or father or children or fields for my sake and for the sake of the gospel, who will not receive a hundred times more, now at this time— houses, brothers and sisters, mothers and children, and fields, with persecutions—and eternal life in the age to come."

In this setting I hardly know what to say. *Who am I to share anything?* I wonder. Sure, I have been to seminary, written books, pastored churches, and led ministries, but compared to these brothers and sisters, I know so little of what it costs to follow Christ. Compared to them, I know so little of what it means to depend on and trust in Christ for all that I need. I know so little of what it means to take risks to make his love known.

Nevertheless, trusting that God's Word is sufficient to encourage them, I open up to Nehemiah 8 and 2 Timothy 4, and I exhort them to hold fast to God's Word, even when it's hard to do so. They nod their heads as Nabin translates. I hope they are encouraged.

It's not until I finish, however, that I am most encouraged. After our time in God's Word, they begin to share their needs with one another. One older woman in the corner of the room mentions a physical challenge she is facing, and a woman on the other side of the room offers to help take care of her. A young man tells of someone he recently shared the gospel with who is now persecuting him, threatening to harm his family. In response, an older man shares how the same thing happened to him, prompting the pastor to encourage them both based on his own experiences with persecution. That leads to a couple who tell about how they shared the gospel with another family and how that family believed in Jesus. They are now thinking about starting a new church in that family's home in a nearby village.

As I watch what is happening in this room and listen to these conversations between brothers and sisters in the family of God, it hits me: This is it! This is what these villages and the people in them need most! Absolutely, they need the gospel. Without question, they need to hear the good news of God's grace that gives them eternal life. But they need more than that, too. They need community—the kind of community that treks for two hours—not just to worship with one another but to care for and encourage one another. The kind of community that takes responsibility for one another's physical needs. They need brothers and sisters who, as we read in Mark 10, provide for one another as family and love one another as themselves (Luke 10). And these villages need a community of men and women who will take great personal risk to share the greatest news in the world with people who have never heard it.

In other words, these villages and the people in them need the church. The church as God has designed it to be. A people fearlessly holding on to God's Word while selflessly sacrificing to share and show God's love amid need around them.

This kind of church can change the world!

It's surprisingly simple when you think about it. Not easy, but simple. This church has so little of the things you and I think about when it comes to church in our culture. They don't have a nice building. They don't have a great band. They don't have a charismatic preacher. They don't have any programs. They just have each other, God's Word in front of them, and God's Spirit among them. And, apparently, that's enough.

I wonder if that would be enough for us. I wonder if that would be enough for me. Would you and I be content with belonging to a community that is simply committed to seeking God, loving each other, and sharing the good news of God's love with the world around us no matter what it costs us? Isn't this the essence of the church according to God's design?

As I sit in the middle of this family of brothers and sisters on this remote mountainside, I can't help but think of how easy it is to get caught up in so much extra stuff in the church that we miss the essence of who God has called us to be and what he has called us to do. I think about what I read in Luke 11 earlier before dinner. There, Jesus confronts the leaders of God's people because they were missing God's design for their community. One verse in particular sticks out:

> Woe to you Pharisees! You give a tenth of mint, rue, and every kind of herb, and you bypass justice and love for God. These things you should have done without neglecting the others. (verse 42)

Jesus indicts the religious leaders because they were so focused on small things, including their traditions (which weren't all bad), that they missed the most important things in God's Word—namely, the spread of God's love and justice. And I wonder if the same indictment could be made against church leaders like me, and the church culture you and I are a part of. Isn't it so easy for us to focus on small things in the church, including our traditions (which aren't all bad), that we miss the most important things—namely, working for justice among the oppressed and loving people in need as we love ourselves?

In light of all the faces of urgent spiritual and physical need

I've seen in just the last few days, I long to be a part of a church like this. I want to be part of a community that is simply committed to the most important things: caring for the hurting with compassion and spreading God's love to the hopeless with courage. I want to be a part of a people who are fearlessly holding on to God's Word while selflessly sacrificing to share and show God's love amid urgent needs in our world. I want to be part of the church like God has designed it to be. The kind of church that can change the world.

As these thoughts flood my mind, the pastor asks me to pray for this church at the close of our gathering. Of course, I'm honored. But I'm also humbled, because I know I'm the one in this room who has the most to learn.

So I pray, boldly,

*God, please show yourself strong on behalf of these brothers and sisters. I pray that you will indeed provide for all their needs. I pray that you will help them hold fast to your Word amid opposition. And I pray that you will help them to spread your love in villages all throughout these mountains amid persecution. And God, I pray that you will help those of us visiting here tonight and the churches we're a part of back home to join with our brothers and sisters here in being the church you have called and created us to be. In Jesus's name, amen.*

# Reflections

What might look different in your life if you were loving people in need as much as you love yourself? In what ways do you justify not loving people in need like this?

What small (even good) things do you and/or your church focus on that keep you from concentrating on the most important things?

What bold prayers are you ready to pray?

# *Day 5:* Nurses, Teachers, and Trout-Poop Experts

## Entrusted with Much

Finally, a new change of clothes! Freshly encouraged and exhilarated after meeting with the church the night before, I decide the next morning four days is sufficient for one set of layers, so it's time on this trek to retire them for another. I trust that the new set will last the final three days. Besides, Aaron told us last night that we'd be hiking mostly downhill today, descending to lower elevation the rest of the way, which means warmer temperatures on the trails. There will even be times when short sleeves will do, because we'll be sweating so much.

Feeling fresh for the day in my new set of clothes, I lie down on my sleeping bag to read Luke 12. As I journal, my attention is drawn specifically to two parables:

> He told them a parable: "A rich man's land was very productive. He thought to himself, 'What should I do, since I don't have anywhere to store my crops? I will do this,' he said. 'I'll tear down my barns and build bigger ones and store all my grain and my goods there. Then I'll say to myself, "You have many goods stored up for many years. Take it easy; eat, drink, and enjoy yourself."'
>
> "But God said to him, 'You fool! This very night your life is demanded of you. And the things you have prepared—whose will they be?'
>
> "That's how it is with the one who stores up treasure for himself and is not rich toward God." (verses 16–21)

*What a stark contrast between where I'm lying right now and where I live back home. I'm surrounded by a barren land, not a bountiful one. It's a battle every day here to meet one's needs. No one is building larger barns to store extra goods. No one has a savings account or 401(k) to depend on in difficult times. Meanwhile, stability and success in my culture is actually defined by bigger barns. Bigger homes to accommodate all our possessions. Bigger bank accounts to make sure we're okay in every* conceivable circumstance. This way, we can relax and enjoy all that this world has to offer.

Yet God labels such a way of life as foolishness. Storing up more possessions and more pleasures in the world is a recipe for wasting one's life. If you really want to be rich, be generous toward God and others. This is the wise way to live.

The Lord said: "Who then is the faithful and sensible manager his master will put in charge of his household servants to give them their allotted food at the proper time? Blessed is that servant whom the master finds doing his job when he comes. Truly I tell you, he will put him in charge of all his possessions. But if that servant says in his heart, 'My master is delaying his coming,' and starts to beat the male and female servants, and to eat and drink and get drunk, that servant's master will come on a day he does not expect him and at an hour he does not know. He will cut him to pieces and assign him a place with the unfaithful. And that servant who knew his master's will and didn't prepare himself or do it will be severely beaten. But the one who did not know and did what deserved punishment will receive a light beating. From everyone who has been given much, much will be required; and from the one who has been entrusted with much, even more will be expected. (verses 42–48)

As I read this last verse, I'm struck again by how much I've been given. How can I even begin to express the wealth God has granted me ever since the day I was born? Not for one day of my life have I ever had to worry about having clean water or sufficient food. I've had all the clothing and shelter I've ever needed. I've never lacked medicine when I've been sick. I've had access to the highest levels of education in the world.

Ever since I needed one, I've had an income sufficient for covering not only my needs but seemingly endless wants. On top of all these things, I've had a mom and dad, a family and friends, who have loved and cared for me my entire life. And more important than everything else, I've known the gospel and had a relationship with God for as long as I can remember.

This well-known scripture "to whom much was given" is surely an apt description of my life. And that means the conclusion is unavoidable. "Of him much will be required."

O God, what do you want me to do? What do you want my family to do? I'll do whatever. Yet even as I pray this, I know I am so prone to prioritize my own wants. To pursue my own plans and my own pleasures. O God, please

*help me do whatever you want me to do with
all you've given me.*

## The Left Fork

After breakfast, we strap on our packs and begin the hike down this mountain toward a village we can see in a distant valley in the district of Nujiang. Hiking downhill, while not as taxing on your muscles as going uphill, causes extra strain on your joints. With every step, you can feel mounting pressure in your ankles and knees. It also increases the possibility of slipping. You might think a particular rock to step on is stable, but sometimes that's not the case, and before you know it, you fall and meet the ground unpleasantly.

At one point we reach a fork in the trail, and Nabin, who's leading the way, tells us that both routes end up at the same place a few hundred feet farther down the mountain. So I ask, "Which one is faster?"

"The one on the left."

At this point, Aaron catches up and, hearing the end of our conversation, says, "That's what Nabin thinks, but I think the one on the right is quicker."

"Aaron doesn't know what he's talking about," Nabin responds with a smile.

Now, I'm a competitive guy, and I can sense an opportunity for competition when I see one. So I ask, "Why don't we race, then? Nabin and I will take the one on the left, and you guys can take the one on the right. We'll see who gets there first."

Aaron smiles and agrees, as does Nabin. For me, it's one of those times when I set something up without really thinking it through. I'm having a hard enough time walking gingerly down this mountain, and I've just volunteered to sprint down this part of it? And I know myself well enough to realize that I'm in this to win, which means I won't necessarily be careful. But I'm already committed.

"On your mark, get set, go!" says Aaron, starting the race.

We're off, Aaron's team veering right as Nabin and I run left. I realize quickly that Nabin has done this many times before. He knows where to step and not step, so I try to mimic his every move. As our momentum increases, so does my anxiety. We are hurtling downhill and I have no idea how we're going to stop.

My fear materializes as I see Nabin suddenly put the brakes on by grabbing a branch above him to stop his momentum, so I do the same as best as I can. And that's when I realize why such an abrupt stop was necessary: Nabin and I are now standing at the top of a small cliff.

Later I'll find out that this cliff is why Nabin thinks this trail is the faster route—because the only way down is to jump and slide down the steep slope on the loose rock. If I'd known about this, I would have gladly swallowed my hubris and followed Aaron. But it's too late now and I don't want to lose.

"You'll be fine," Nabin says, no doubt seeing the concern on my face. "Just do what I do."

Nabin quickly jumps and slides down, easily staying on his feet. I follow his lead. Let's just say I didn't make it look easy, and I didn't stay on my feet! But I made it, and that's all that matters.

"Come on," Nabin says, "we're almost there."

I pick myself up off the ground and run behind him. The last thing I want is to have jumped down a cliff in vain, only to lose a race. Winning now is everything!

So Nabin and I run as fast as we can down the second half of this trail. I'm a wild man now! Something about jumping and sliding down a cliff successfully removes all fear of anything else to come. Before we know it, we arrive at a clearing. No one else is there. "We did it! We beat them," Nabin says, a smile spreading across his face.

I laugh too. Scant seconds later Aaron and Chris round the corner, with Sigs and all his gear not too far behind.

That's when Aaron shares with me about the cliff . . . and why he always avoids the left fork in the trail.

*Thanks.*

## Health Outpost

Although on the top of the mountain we could see the village in the distance, it takes a few hours of trekking for us to arrive there. We stop at the first building we come to, and Aaron invites us to step inside.

"Let me introduce you to Maya," he says as he turns to a woman in her early thirties dressed in medical scrubs. "Maya grew up in the capital. She finished secondary school and then went to university to study nursing. Now she has moved up to this village to provide medical care."

Maya smiles shyly.

Aaron explains that before Maya came here, there was no medical care available for miles. If anyone became sick in several villages nearby, the person would have to walk miles down the mountains toward the city to get help.

"That obviously means people had to be healthy enough to make that walk," Aaron says. "If they couldn't make the trek, they couldn't get the care."

As Maya was finishing her university studies, Aaron asked her if she would be willing to move up into this remote village to run a health outpost he was starting. "Maya had many options," Aaron explains, "and every other option would have paid more money and offered more comfort. But she chose to come up here."

Maya, blushing at the attention given her, softly says, "I just want to do what God wants me to do with what God has given to me."

Hearing her say that, I remember my prayer earlier that morning. Her words are almost exactly what I'd prayed: "God, please help me do whatever you want me to do with all you've given me."

Now I find myself thinking, *Would I be willing to do this? If I were in Maya's shoes, would I come up here alone, sacrificing all sorts of comforts and opportunities to advance a career, in order to serve people in this distant, remote village?* I'd like to think my answer would be yes, but I'm not so sure.

"Will you show them around the outpost?" Aaron asks Maya.

"I would be glad to," she replies, and we begin the tour. It lasts all of two rooms, one she calls the pharmacy. Shelves are lined with all sorts of medicines that she and Aaron have worked hard to obtain for patients who need them. These include basic vaccines and simple remedies for common sicknesses. "We're trying to increase the volume of our stock," Maya explains, "for the more villagers we are able to help, the more others travel from remote areas to get the medicine."

Then Maya leads us into the examination room, where she meets patients. There's a small, plain wooden table in the middle of the room for a patient to sit or lie on. A few medical tools rest beside it. There's also a file cabinet for Maya to keep her patient records. As she talks about her work, Maya beams with humble joy over the difference she has seen this outpost make in many people's lives, not only physically but also spiritually. "They have so many physical needs," Maya says, "yet I know that their greatest need is spiritual."

I nod as I watch and listen to this sweet sister in Christ completely solve the tension I have wrestled with between sharing the gospel and doing social ministry. It's never occurred to Maya to disconnect these two emphases. Maya knows she is surrounded by urgent physical needs, and she is working hard day in and day out alone in this village to help bring about physical healing. At the same time, Maya knows that everyone's greatest need is far deeper than what any medicine or treatment could ever provide, so she's willing to lay down her life to proclaim the gospel so that more people might experience healing in their hearts.

Before we leave, I thank Maya for the example she is to me of what it means to do whatever God calls us to do and to do it with joy and delight. With this, we gather around Maya and pray for her and the health outpost.

We walk outside and shoulder our packs, not realizing that

meeting Maya is just the beginning of similar encounters today with men and women who will challenge, convict, and encourage us by their examples.

## More Than Education

We continue into the village, and between the trail and the river, we come to a school comprised of four rectangular buildings, with a courtyard in the middle where students can congregate for outdoor activities.

We veer off the trail, and Aaron tells us to set our packs down. At the first building, we hear children's voices coming from inside the classrooms. Aaron invites us to step in and observe the first one we come to.

There we find about thirty kids seated on four long benches. Our presence in the room creates an immediate disruption as the students turn to look at us. They start whispering and pointing to us, smiling and laughing. Their teachers, one born in this country and one who moved here from another country, attempt to regain their attention and ask them to greet us as guests in their language. Then the teachers suggest that the kids sing a song they recently learned, and the children happily oblige. As their faces light up the room and their voices fill the air, complete with accompanying hand motions, I immediately think about my wife. Heather's an elementary-school teacher, and she would love to be here right now.

We make our way to the other buildings, through the other classrooms, where similar scenes play out. We then come to the fourth building, which is not a classroom but a dormitory and kitchen.

"Do the kids sleep here?" I ask Nabin.

"No, they hike back and forth every day from their villages."

"Then who lives here?" I ask.

"The teachers," Nabin responds. "None of these teachers are from this village. All the Asian teachers completed their schooling in the city at the base of the mountains and then chose to come up here and work in this school we were starting."

As I listen, the parallels with Maya's life are obvious.

"And as you noticed," Nabin adds, "there are also teachers from other countries. They, of course, did their studies elsewhere and then moved here to teach."

As I listen to Nabin, I walk around the room. There's an area with bunk beds for female teachers, a separate area with bunk beds for male teachers, and one more area separated off for a husband and wife who live and teach there. The few clothes and possessions each teacher has are organized neatly around their bunks.

In the small kitchen, the teachers cook their breakfast and dinner, as well as lunch for the students and themselves. Across the way is a small outhouse with two in-ground toilets (or, as some people call them, squatty potties), as well as another room for bathing.

"This is not an easy way to live," I say out loud, not thinking about anyone being around me.

"They didn't move up here because they thought it would be easy," Nabin hears me and replies.

With that, we step back outside into the courtyard, where all the kids are now coming for recess. I watch as these kids run and play. This is no rest time for the teachers, as the children dance around them and jump onto their backs and into their arms to be carried and swung around. As I watch the kids smile, giggle, laugh, and play, I see teachers who believe these kids and their families are worth what it takes to live here.

Aaron comes to me and says, "Before this school was built, these kids had nothing. And even once it was built, we had to find teachers, which was not an easy task. But God provided. And now, for the first time, these kids have access to education.

"And teaching is just the beginning," Aaron continues. "Because these teachers love these kids, they get to know their families, too. As they do, they learn about more needs in the community, and they work with the health outpost or others to care for those needs. And in the middle of it all—"

"Let me guess," I interrupt Aaron. "They're focused on people's greatest need, which is the gospel."

"You're catching on." Aaron laughs. "These teachers are passionate about both physical need [in this case, education] and spiritual need [in every case, the gospel]. They don't choose between the two, even while they prioritize the spiritual. They know education is huge for opening up all kinds of opportunities. But they also know that education alone won't open eternal life."

## Trout and Vegetables

As the recess ends and the kids go back to their classrooms, Aaron says, "I want to introduce you to someone else at the teahouse up ahead." So we grab our packs and follow him back onto the trail.

When we arrive at the teahouse, we walk inside and sit at the table for a late lunch (or, really, an early dinner, as this is where we're staying tonight). We order the usual: lentil soup, bread, and (you guessed it) masala tea. A few minutes later, a thick, bearded, brawny Caucasian man, whom I guess to be in his early sixties, enters.

"Ben!" Aaron shouts, smiling, before the two men shake hands and slap each other on the back.

Aaron turns and introduces each of us to Ben. After Ben and Aaron sit down, we listen in as they catch up with each other briefly. Ben tells how his wife, Annie, is doing well here in the community, and his two daughters, who have finished college back in the States, are doing great. After more conversation between them, Aaron turns and says to us, "Listen, I want you all to hear what Ben does. He and his wife moved up to this village not long ago and are making a big difference in a unique way. Ben, please don't be shy," Aaron says as he turns toward him. "Tell them all about you, trout poop, and the gospel."

That piques our curiosity!

"Well," Ben begins, with a deep southern drawl, "I've been involved in agricultural engineering all my life back in the South . . . the southern US, that is" (as if we thought he might be originally from southern Asia). "But then I came on a trip out here with Aaron, and I saw the need for food in these villages. The soil isn't good for growing vegetables, but that led me to start thinking about ways I could help.

"So I planned another time to come back up here, and I set up a little experiment. I put some fish in a small tank with water and engineered some PVC pipes to cycle water from the tank to a platform with plants. Then I engineered that water to recycle back into the fish tank after its exposure to the plants. It's called aquaponics."

He has our total interest—none of us thought we would encounter something like this in such a remote village.

"It starts with fish poop," Ben says with passion. "The waste from the fish gets released into the water. Their waste is rich in nitrate, which is the form of nitrogen that plants use to grow. So basically the fish poop turns into plant food. And as the plants eat the food, they clean the water for the fish, which then recycles back around for the fish to live in. So the fish and the plants help each other grow, and you have a continual supply of food and vegetables."

"I love that. How creative," Sigs says.

"The experiment worked well the first time, but we needed to make some changes. So I came back on a third trip, this time with my wife, and we tried to use solar power to sustain the system. We were able to get that to work, and we also learned we could use bamboo as the medium to pump the water through. The plant yield was amazing, even though we were doing this on a pretty small scale. And we could see what a difference this could make for people in these villages."

"I can't tell you how excited I was with what happened next!" Aaron says.

"That's when my wife and I decided that God was calling us here," Ben concludes. "Since God has given me the ability to create these kinds of systems, and people here who don't have enough food could live and thrive if I just used what God has given me, we decided coming here was a no-brainer."

## Unique Gifts

While I listen to Ben, Luke 12:48 comes back to my mind: "To whom much was given, of him much will be required" (ESV).

Others around the table start asking Ben questions about how aquaponics works. A couple of sentences in, my focus drifts, because I'm totally enamored by Ben's example.

I think about my own life. I definitely don't have skills in agricultural engineering, and I could never do what Ben is doing. My wife can testify to my complete uselessness when it comes to anything outdoors: fishing, hunting, gardening, construction . . . literally anything outdoors. But that's the great thing about listening to Ben. He and I have totally different education, experiences, gifts, and passions, but we each have a unique part to play in using what God has given us for spreading his love and meeting the world's urgent needs.

And *unique* is the right word. Here I sit with years of seminary training and ministry-leadership experience, both of which I want to use for God's glory in the world. But in this moment, I am looking at this brother in Christ who, as far as I know, has no seminary training or formal ministry-leadership experience. Yet he's thriving in work here with these people in a way that I clearly never could.

To take that a step further, it would be nearly impossible for me to get a visa to even live in this country with my credentials.

Governments in countries like this, where the gospel hasn't gone, often work to keep pastors and missionaries away. But people like Ben have an open invitation because of the skills and assistance they bring.

I recall another man I met recently on a plane. He recognized me from some Bible-study videos and started a conversation. His name was Hugh, and he was from Demopolis, Alabama (think small town, sweet home Alabama). I asked Hugh where he was flying, and he told me he was headed to Mexico for his lumber business. I asked him if that business had expanded into any other countries, and he started telling me that they were now working across East Asia and Southeast Asia and were looking to expand into the Middle East.

As I remember that conversation, I wonder if Hugh has ever thought about how God is opening these doors, not just for the spread of lumber through his work but for the spread of the gospel through his life.

That brings another man to mind, whose story is strangely similar to Ben's (both stories involve waste!). This man has a horse-bedding business, also in Alabama. He's been particularly success-ful because in northern Alabama there's a certain tree with wood uniquely able to soak up a horse's urine, so it makes for good horse bedding. One day I was sitting in a meeting with this man and other business leaders who were exploring different avenues for expanding business in the Middle East that might aid the spread of the gospel there. As we looked at a list of potential industries, horse bedding was one of them. This man's eyes lit up: he saw the potential of his horse bedding advancing the cause of Christ in the

Middle East! I laughed as I thought about the creativity of God—how in his sovereignty he had designed a tree in northern Alabama to uniquely soak up horse urine for the spread of the gospel in the Middle East.

My mind floods with other examples. I think about friends who moved to North Africa, where they now have a booming rug business. They travel into villages and buy antique North African rugs and then pay to have them repaired and cleaned. In this way they help provide financial support for people in these villages while also opening opportunities to share the gospel with them.

I put all this together and can't help but wonder if God has designed the globalization of today's marketplace to open up avenues for the spread of the gospel around the world. And I can't help but believe that God has given all kinds of people unique education, experiences, gifts, and passions that can be used in ways we've never imagined.

What if we thought that way as Christians? What if we all thought like Ben thinks? What if each of us really considered all the ways we might play a unique part in the spread of the gospel where it has not yet gone?

## Salt and Light

At this point, Sigs speaks up. "Listening to you, Ben, makes me wonder how I can use photography to work around the world for the spread of the gospel."

"If trout poop can be used like this, I would think photography can be too," Ben replies.

Aaron jumps in. "Just think of what would happen if followers of Christ were taking advantage of opportunities like this." That leads to a discussion of different ways followers of Jesus can play a part.

We talk about high school students who will pay money or get scholarships to attend a college or university somewhere. What if those students started looking for opportunities to go to school in countries where the gospel is scarce? I share about an article I read about many colleges and universities overseas that will give American students a full scholarship for a degree program (in English-speaking classes).

Chris says, "What a difference it would make if high school students didn't just think about a future school in terms of their favorite football team or what seems coolest or most comfortable to them but instead thought about where they could study while spreading the gospel to people who have never heard it."

Then Sigs tells about some students he's heard say they want to quit school and work for justice in the world. But what many students fail to recognize is the plethora of opportunities to work for justice as a result of getting a degree. "After all," Sigs says, "we met teachers earlier today who are investing their lives in these kids not because they quit their education but because they completed their education with excellence."

He continues, "I know of a young woman who got her university degree in nursing and then started looking overseas for job opportunities. That led her to the Middle East, where she started working in a strategic hospital in a large city. Today she is head of nursing in that hospital and has regular Bible studies in her office. Nobody stops her, because she's so good at nursing."

This story makes me wonder what would happen if students worked hard to get degrees so that the nations would clamor for them to come and doors would open up for the spread of the gospel where it hasn't gone.

"It's not just students or professionals," Ben says. "Now that I'm in my sixties, I think about retirement and how Uncle Sam's money can be used not just for golf in Florida but for the spread of the gospel in other countries."

I share about one country in Southeast Asia that is offering major financial incentives now to entice Westerners to retire there. That country has millions of people who have never heard the gospel. "What might happen," I ask, "if Christians—maybe even a group from the same church—chose to retire in that country to both enjoy their latter years together and also represent Jesus to the lost?"

As we talk, it's clear that Ben's example has broadened our understanding of opportunities to be light and salt to the "ends of the earth" (Psalm 65:5). I wonder what would happen if more Bens, including you and me, took Luke 12:48 seriously.

## Ultimate Treasure

After we eat, Ben takes us to the trout farm. There we meet Ben's wife, Annie, and together they show us how everything works. Indeed, trout poop is far more fascinating than one might originally think.

Then we all walk back up to the teahouse, where we're joined by Maya and the other teachers from the school for a time of prayer. Aaron asks me to share something with all of us from the Word, so I turn to Luke 12, the same passage I read earlier this morning. I read aloud the following words from Jesus:

> Fear not, little flock, for it is your Father's good pleasure
> to give you the kingdom. Sell your possessions, and give
> to the needy. Provide yourselves with moneybags that
> do not grow old, with a treasure in the heavens that does
> not fail, where no thief approaches and no moth destroys.
> For where your treasure is, there will your heart be also.
> (verses 32–34, ESV)

As I share with the group, I point out how Jesus is not telling his disciples ultimately to sacrifice treasure in their lives. Instead, he's encouraging them to seek ultimate treasure in their lives—the kind that will last forever. He's exhorting them to live for long-term treasure they can never lose, not short-term treasure they can never keep.

This is the exact opposite of the way the world thinks and works. We want gratification, and we want it now. We want to make the most of this life now (we even market Christianity as the key to our best life now). But it sure seems as though Jesus's message sounds more like our best lives later. And forever. Jesus is actually telling his disciples to give away their possessions in this world now and give to those in need in a way that will lead to eternal pleasure in a heavenly kingdom.

There's almost a tinge of self-serving motivation in Jesus's words, isn't there? When you think about it, this passage is not really a call to sacrifice as much as it is a call to satisfaction. Jesus is calling his followers to gain as much ultimate treasure as possible.

This, I share with the group, is the picture I see at work in their lives. All of them have done this. They have forsaken all sorts of pleasures in this world to live and work in this place. They have sold and given away all sorts of possessions. They have laid aside various pursuits and pleasures. But one thing is clear: they are living for treasure. Ultimate treasure. They are living for the kind of treasure that will last forever.

I pause and look at the faces around me. I think about the prayer I wrote at the beginning of the day:

*O God, please help me do whatever you want me to do with all you've given me.*

Now at the end of the day, I am seeing a circle of men and women from their twenties to their sixties, and they are doing whatever God has called them to do with all he has given them. So I simply encourage them: "As you work in that health outpost, as you teach those kids, as you work that aquaponics system, and as you share the gospel with people all around you, you may wonder some days if it's worth it. You may wonder some days if it's worth the sacrifices you are making and the challenges you are enduring. And I just want to remind you, straight from the mouth of Jesus, that it's worth it. You are living for what lasts. And there is nothing in this world that even comes close to comparing with the treasure you are storing up not only for yourselves but for men, women, and children all over these mountains."

As the words leave my mouth, they boomerang back to my own heart, because I want to live for treasure like this. Indeed, I want to do all Jesus has called me to do with all God has given me to do it.

After I close in prayer and we all say good night, I can't get to my room soon enough. There I unpack my things, pull out my journal, and write,

> O God, I want to use whatever gifts you have
> given me for the spread of your gospel in the
> world. I want to use all you have entrusted to
> me to store up treasure that will last forever.
> So what do you want me to do? Do you want
> me to move to a place like this? Are you calling
> me to give my life among these people, making
> disciples and training pastors? In some ways, it
> seems like a no-brainer: move here! There's so
> little gospel, so few churches, so few pastors, and
> so much need. So much opportunity for storing up
> eternal treasure! Why would I not come here?
> The only way I can imagine not coming here is if
> I'm doing more in the US to affect what's going
> on here than if I were actually living here.
> O God, please lead and guide me—and Heather
> and our kids—by your Spirit, according to your

*will. I want to do all you call me to do with all you've given me to do it. Jesus, I want to live for real, lasting, never-ending, ever-satisfying treasure! Amen.*

## Reflections

"From everyone who has been given much, much will be required; and from the one who has been entrusted with much, even more will be expected" (Luke 12:48). What comes to your mind personally when you read this verse?

Thinking creatively, what opportunities exist around you right now to use your God-given, unique gifts to affect others in need and spread gospel hope? How could those same gifts be used in places far from where you live?

# Day 6: Like a King Preparing for War

## A Superior Love

I wake up this morning feeling tense. Not that this trip hasn't already had its fair share of tension, but last night I went to bed wondering if God is calling me to move to this country and serve here. That made for restless sleep.

So this morning I have countless questions about what that would mean. And the questions aren't just mine. I'm thinking about all the questions Heather's going to ask me when I wonder aloud with her whether God could be leading us to move here. I'm thinking about what all this might mean for my wife, my kids, and our future.

Needing to hear the Word of God, I open up my Bible to Luke 13–14. My morning reading ends with these words:

> Great crowds were traveling with him. So he turned and said to them: "If anyone comes to me and does not hate his own father and mother, wife and children, brothers and sisters—yes, and even his own life—he cannot be my disciple. Whoever does not bear his own cross and come after me cannot be my disciple.
>
> "For which of you, wanting to build a tower, doesn't first sit down and calculate the cost to see if he has enough to complete it? Otherwise, after he has laid the foundation and cannot finish it, all the onlookers will begin to ridicule him, saying, 'This man started to build and wasn't able to finish.'
>
> "Or what king, going to war against another king, will not first sit down and decide if he is able with ten thousand to oppose the one who comes against him with twenty thousand? If not, while the other is still far off, he sends a delegation and asks for terms of peace. In the same way, therefore, every one of you who does not renounce all his possessions cannot be my disciple.
>
> "Now, salt is good, but if salt should lose its taste, how will it be made salty? It isn't fit for the soil or for the

manure pile; they throw it out. Let anyone who has ears to hear listen." (14:25–35)

I've preached and written on this passage before, but these words take on entirely new meaning as I sit here reflecting on the possibility of my family following Jesus by moving to this part of the world. I remember one of my favorite quotes on this passage from pastor and author John Stott. In his words:

> The Christian landscape is strewn with the wreckage of derelict, half-built towers—the ruins of those who began to build and were unable to finish. All too many people still ignore Christ's warning and undertake to follow him without first pausing to reflect on the cost of doing so. The result is the great scandal of so-called nominal Christianity. In countries to which Christian civilization has spread, large numbers of people have covered themselves with a decent, but thin, veneer of Christianity. They have allowed themselves to become a little bit involved; enough to be respectable but not enough to be uncomfortable. Their religion is a great, soft cushion. It protects them from the hard unpleasantness of life, while changing its place and shape to suit their convenience. No wonder cynics complain of hypocrites in the church and dismiss religion as escapism.*

---

* John Stott, *Basic Christianity* (Downers Grove, IL: InterVarsity, 2008), 144–45.

Reading Luke 14 now, I'm reminded of how easily I can shape my religion to suit my convenience. So am I really willing to follow Jesus wherever and however he leads me, no matter what that means for me or my family? According to Jesus, following him requires a love for him so supreme that it makes love for even our family look like hate in comparison.

I remember the seventeenth-century preacher John Bunyan. Authorities threatened to throw him in prison if he did not stop preaching. Bunyan knew that if he went to prison, his wife and children (one of whom was blind) would be left destitute. Even when he was a free man his family had little food or clothing. His imprisonment would mean their impoverishment. Yet Jesus had called him to preach the gospel, so he could not stay silent. He was subsequently imprisoned, where he wrote the following from his cell:

> The parting with my wife and poor children, hath often
> been to me in this place, as the pulling the flesh from my
> bones, and that not only because I am somewhat too
> fond of these great mercies, but also because I should
> have often brought to my mind the many hardships,
> miseries, and wants that my poor family was like to meet
> with, should I be taken from them, especially my poor
> blind child, who lay nearer my heart than all besides:
> Oh! the thoughts of the hardship I thought my poor
> blind one might go under, would break my heart to
> pieces. . . . But yet recalling myself, thought I, I must

venture you all with God, though it goeth to the quick
to leave you: Oh! I saw in this condition I was a man
who was pulling down his house upon the head of his
wife and children; yet, thought I, I must do it, I must
do it.*

As if superior love were not enough, Jesus goes on to say that
he requires one's entire life. Devotion to Jesus means denial of
oneself and death to one's thoughts, desires, plans, and dreams.
According to Jesus, following him means making him your entire life.

So I write,

*Jesus, you are my entire life. Whatever you
want me to do, I want to do. Including moving
here. What would this look like for me and for
my family? Please help me to count the cost of
what that might mean. O God, I want to
renounce everything in this world that you
want me to renounce. I don't want to shape
my Christianity to suit my convenience! Please
guide my steps, and please guard me from myself
every step of the way. Please lead me by your
Spirit however you desire, I pray!*

---

* John Bunyan, *Grace Abounding to the Chief of Sinners* (Welwyn Garden City, UK:
Evangelical Press, 1978), 123.

## Spiritual Warfare

After packing up my things, I make my way to the teahouse, where I sit down at the breakfast table next to Chris and Nabin, across from Aaron and Sigs. As we eat our usual morning meal, Chris asks me where I was in my Bible reading that morning. I share about the end of Luke 14 and the importance of counting the cost of following Christ in this world, like a builder preparing to construct a tower or like a king preparing to go to war.

Then I ask Aaron, "When you decided to give your life doing ministry in challenging circumstances like these, how did you count that cost? How did you measure what the work here was going to take?"

"That's a great question," Aaron says. "We knew that physically, work in such remote mountains would be hard for obvious reasons. But we learned very quickly that the physical challenges were nothing compared to the spiritual challenges."

"How'd you learn that?" Chris asks.

"Well," he says, "when we first came up to these villages and started sharing the gospel, we were immediately told to leave and never come back. In fact, a few people threatened to kill us if we tried to come back."

"Why?" Sigs asks.

"There's a strong belief here that you need to appease various gods or spirits in order for things to go well for you. And if anyone disrupts the stability of worship for those gods or spirits, then bad things can happen to a village. As a result, when people found out we were followers of Jesus, they believed we were introducing a foreign, competing god who would upset their gods, so they wanted us gone."

"That's frightening," Chris says.

"And you know," Aaron goes on, "there's a sense in which they were exactly right. Based on what the Bible says about spiritual warfare, there is absolutely a false god named the devil who has been deceiving minds and hearts for centuries among these people. He has kept Jesus from being proclaimed as the one true God here for generations, and he will do whatever he can to keep that from changing."

Aaron pauses, as if he's reluctant to share something. I can tell something specific is on his mind, so I ask him, "How have you seen that play out?"

He takes a deep breath and says, "Let me tell you a story that I probably wouldn't believe if I hadn't been a part of it. But it will give you some perspective on the spiritual war that is waging here."

"Okay, we're listening."

"One day," Aaron starts, "I was hiking through a nearby village. I hadn't been here long, and it was my first time to ever be in that particular village. As I was hiking, all of a sudden a woman, maybe in her midthirties, came running by me really fast. She startled me because she seemed out of control, and I could sense that something was wrong with her. She ran ahead, though, and I lost sight of her.

"A few minutes later," Aaron continues, "the trail led me right next to where this woman's house was apparently located. As I got near the house, I saw this same woman dart out of her front door. She had a crazed look on her face and a bottle in her hand, which

I later found out was insecticide. She stood there in front of her door facing me as I walked toward her on the trail, and she started shouting. I stopped in my tracks, totally stunned and unsure of what was happening.

"That's when the woman yelled in the local dialect, in a manner that seemed like she was possessed by something demonic, 'This is your welcome to our villages,' and she took the bottle in her hand and started drinking it. I didn't know what was in the bottle, but I immediately got concerned when her husband came running out of the house with their kids, all yelling, 'No! No! No!' But by the time they got to her, she had swallowed almost everything in the bottle. At that point, she started convulsing and gasping for breath. The husband started yelling for help, so I dropped my pack and ran straight to them. She seemed to be losing consciousness, and before long, she wasn't breathing. I started trying to revive her, but nothing was working. Within a matter of minutes, she was dead."

We sit silently at the breakfast table, trying to imagine this scene.

"It was one of the worst moments of my entire life," Aaron says. "To see a woman kill herself in front of her husband and children. And to do it because I came hiking into this village."

"Did you even know this woman?" Sigs asks.

"No," Aaron answers, "I'd never been in this village, and I'd never met this woman. The first time I ever saw her was when she came running by me on the trail."

Aaron pauses again and then continues. "That's when I knew that the physical battles of hunger and sickness in these villages pale in comparison to the spiritual battle for people's hearts and minds. And I had to ask the question, Was I ready for that kind of battle?"

As Sigs and Chris ask Aaron more questions, my mind immediately goes back to whether or not God is calling me and my family to live here. *Am I ready for this kind of spiritual war?* I wonder. And not just me. I think about all the opportunities we discussed yesterday for students, professionals, and retirees to spread the gospel around the world. Indeed, that's no light commitment.

*Like a king preparing for war, there's a cost to be counted.*

## Alisha's Courage

Soon breakfast is over and we're back on the trail, hiking today to a village in Lhuntse, where our plan is to be part of training a small group of pastors and church planters. One of the local teachers from the school we visited yesterday is joining us for today's trek. Her name is Alisha. As we start walking, Aaron quickly catches up to me and says, "At some point in the next couple of hours, you need to ask Alisha about her story. She'll really give you perspective on Luke 14."

Not long after that, the trail widens and I catch up to Alisha. She's in her early twenties, fresh out of completing a teaching degree at a university in the capital. She speaks with a soft voice and has a sweet, shy demeanor that masks the short, hard life she's endured. After a few minutes of conversation about the beauty of this area, I ask Alisha, "Can you tell me about your family?"

"I have an older brother," Alisha says, "who lives in a monastery. My parents sent him there when he was young, and ever since then he's been studying to be a monk."

"Where were you born?"

"A village farther up in the mountains."

"Do your parents still live there?"

"My parents," Alisha starts, but then she pauses. "Well, I probably should go back a little bit. I was born on what my family believed was a 'bad day.' My village was very superstitious, and certain days were seen as evil. And I happened to be born on one of those days.

"My grandfather," she continues, "was a devil talker. People believed he could communicate with the devil. And when I was born on that bad day, my grandfather pronounced that I was born to worship the devil. So from the time I was young, about three or four years old, he told my parents that I needed to give offerings to the devil every day. So my parents built a small room outside our house with an altar to the devil. I can remember as a child having to leave our house every night, walk out to that small room alone in the dark, and give an offering to the devil. Every night," Alisha repeats. "I was very scared."

As I'm listening to her, I think about my youngest son. He's five years old. I picture the smile on his face. And I can't imagine sending him at age three or four out to a dark room alone at night to give an offering to the devil.

"But then one day everything changed in my dad's life," Alisha says. "A blind man came through our village with a guide alongside him. This blind man came into our home, and he told my dad about Jesus. He told my dad that Jesus has authority over the devil and sin. He told my dad that Jesus is the one true God, who came to conquer the devil, sin, and death so that we can be forgiven of our sin and restored to a right relationship with the one true God."

"Had your dad ever heard about Jesus before?" I ask.

"No, this was the first time. But it didn't take long for him to believe in Jesus. He knew that worshipping others gods and spirits, including the devil, was wrong. He was ready to believe in Jesus."

As we walk together, my heart overflows with joy over a blind man who cared enough about the people in this village to bring the gospel to Alisha's dad. I think about how hard it is to trek through these steep, narrow trails with two eyes—what would it be like as a blind man? We just can't make excuses for not getting the gospel to people who haven't heard it.

Alisha continues. "Everything in my dad's life changed. He had a whole new outlook on everything. This blind man gave him a Bible, and he started to read it alone and with our family. Before long my mom believed in Jesus too. And for me, I no longer had to offer worship to the devil. Instead, my dad began teaching me about Jesus."

"How did your grandfather respond to all this?" I ask.

"He was very mad," Alisha says. "And not just him. Everyone in the village was mad. My grandfather and the rest of the villagers believed my dad was introducing a foreign god into the village and that this would bring trouble." As Alisha talks, I realize she is illustrating the resistance to the gospel that Aaron had explained over breakfast. "So in a matter of just a few weeks," she continues, "my family was totally ostracized in the village."

"What do you mean?" I ask.

"We were told we couldn't get water from the well—that we would need to go to another village instead. No one wanted to share a meal or come into our home anymore. We were like outcasts."

As Alisha shares, I can tell this was all terribly painful, but I'm not prepared for what she shares next.

"Then one day," Alisha says, her voice now starting to tremble, "when I was about twelve years old, my mom and dad were out walking on the trail to get water and supplies from another village. They didn't come back, though, and I started to get worried. And that's when our village leaders came to my home. They told me that as my parents were walking back to our village, a landslide occurred. The rocks came tumbling straight toward them, and my mom and dad fell down the mountain and died."

"Alisha, I'm so sorry to hear that." Tears are streaming down her face, and my eyes are watering as well.

She stops talking as she gathers her emotions. I want to give her some time and space, so I don't say anything for a while. After some minutes pass, Alisha breaks the silence.

"But that's not actually what happened to my parents," Alisha says.

"What do you mean?"

"My mom and dad didn't die in a landslide."

Confused, I ask, "Then how did they die?"

Alisha pauses, as if she's afraid to say what's about to come out of her mouth. Then she shares, "The village leaders stoned them."

Stunned silent, I keep listening.

"Years later," Alisha says, wiping tears away, "I learned how village leaders had attacked my mom and dad on the trail that day, pelting them with rocks until they were dead. After this, the leaders pushed my parents' bodies down the mountain. Then they fabricated the story about the landslide and spread the word that just like they'd warned, if you introduce a foreign god into the village, the gods and spirits in the mountains will do bad things to you."

The reality of Alisha's story sets in as she shares, "To this day, whenever anyone talks about Jesus anywhere near my village, people will say, 'Don't worship Jesus. Remember what happened to the only other people who worshipped him here. They died in a landslide.'"

As we continue walking, Alisha tells me how she knew she still wanted to follow Jesus. After being orphaned, she ended up going to a school and home down in the city, where she also found a church to be a part of.

Alisha was extremely nervous about getting baptized, because she knew that would be a more formal, final break from her village and her remaining relatives, including her brother, who was still training in the monastery. But after many conversations with her brother, and after fully counting the cost, a few years ago she was baptized, publicly confessing her faith in Christ. Now, after finishing university, she is teaching up in the village we were in yesterday, working for the spread of the gospel in the mountains where her parents were martyred.

## Dangerous Message

As Alisha and I continue talking, we catch up to the others stopped for a break. We drop our packs and fill up our water bottles, then sit on rocks overlooking the trail.

These are surreal moments, where you sit back and realize where you are and what you're doing. But it's interesting how what awes you changes the farther you walk on these trails. At first you are amazed by the scenery—and don't misunderstand, it's still breathtaking. You still want to take a picture everywhere you turn. But now what's far more amazing are the people around you. You look over at Alisha and Nabin, who grew up in these very mountains. And now that you know their stories, you're just humbled to be walking with them.

After about a half-hour break, we pick up our packs and trek again. "We're not far from the next village," Aaron says, "where we'll spend the rest of the day."

Hearing that this is our last opportunity to hike today, I lag behind a bit to process what I've heard this morning. As I think about the stories Aaron and Alisha have shared, I realize in a fresh way how, if I'm not careful, I can easily have—and even communicate—a romantic view of following Jesus in the world.

I preach sermons and write books and use social media to call people to take the gospel around the world. Yet this morning has been a reminder of what I'm calling people to. To a spiritual battle that could lead to someone's suicide. To work among people who, if they believe what you say, may get stoned for it.

And it's obviously not just others I'm calling to go to tough places. I can't call others to do something I'm not doing myself. As I consider the possibility of moving to this place, I'm not under any illusion that it's easy to live here. Even more so, I'm not under any illusion that life and work are easy here. Indeed, people and places in the world not reached with the gospel are unreached for a reason. They're difficult to reach. They're dangerous to reach. I'm pretty sure all the easy ones are taken.

As I think about living and serving in the hard places in the world, Jesus's words in Luke 14 make more sense to me. I've often wondered why these words of his seem so foreign to me and most every other Christian I've been around in North America, particularly where churches are prevalent. It doesn't feel too costly to follow Christ in America. Sure, it means giving time and money we might spend elsewhere, but we're not in danger of being stoned like Alisha's parents or being abandoned with nothing to our name like the pastor I'd met two nights ago.

But I wonder if that's the disconnect between us and Jesus's words in Luke 14. On one hand, I praise God that I was born into a family where I've heard the gospel since the day I was born. I praise God for parents, friends, and a church who have loved and cared for me so that it didn't cost me my life or possessions to follow Jesus. But if I stop there and keep my life and possessions for myself, then I need to ask the question, Am I really following Jesus?

According to Luke 14, I'm not. Because if I'm truly a Christian, I'm expected to die to my life and my plans in order to follow

Jesus wherever he leads me. And if I'm following him, then inevitably he's going to lead me to people who don't yet know his love. And inevitably he's going to lead me to those who are in urgent need of his provision. And, *inevitably,* that is going to be costly for me.

So, I conclude, the only way to avoid the cost Jesus describes in Luke 14 is not to follow him. Maybe we can call ourselves Christians, but we'll be doing so as we indulge in a world of comfort while ignoring a world of urgent spiritual and physical need. Or maybe giving relative minutes of our time and pennies of our money toward those in need while continuing on with a life that's essentially focused on ourselves.

Regardless of what I have preached or written in the past, I am confronted on this trail with the reality that I am tempted every single day to not follow Jesus as described in Luke 14. I realize that in my life there is a constant lure toward comfort and away from need in the world. That lure is strong, and I need brothers and sisters in Christ like Alisha and Aaron to remind me continually that the life of a Christian is always costly—for people who are actually following Christ.

## The Dal Bhat Buffet

We arrive at the next village, where we'll spend the rest of the day. We set our packs down in rooms, then come together for lunch. On the menu today is dal bhat, a variation on the lentil soup we'd eaten all along the trek.

Picture a silver plate with a mound of white rice in the middle.

Next to it is a silver bowl filled with a brown soupy sauce called dal. Dal contains lentils, vegetable curry, and a variety of spices. To properly dine, you pour the dal over your mound of rice. As the sauce seeps into the rice, you now have a plate of dal bhat.

The hosts at the guesthouse scrounge for spoons to offer you, but the locals don't need spoons. You decide you've now eaten enough meals here to be considered a local, so you shake your head no when a spoon is offered. Eating local means, first, using only your right hand. The left hand is traditionally used for . . . well . . . let's just say "less clean" tasks.

So you lift your right hand and put your middle three fingers together to form a sort of spoon to hold the food. Then you place those fingers under or behind some of the rice that now has dal on it. Once your fingers are under or behind the rice, you use your thumb to slide the dal bhat onto those fingers. Then you lift your hand, with your thumb and fingers holding the food in place, to your mouth, where you insert the food (along with some of your fingers) onto your tongue, where those Asian spices greet you with a hearty hello.

You continue this process until your plate begins to clear, but that doesn't mean you're finished. As soon as the rice and dal on your plate begin to disappear, your host reappears with more rice and more dal. You now realize this is an all-you-can-eat dal bhat buffet. And depending on how the dal bhat is sitting with you, you decide whether or not to go with seconds or even thirds.

As we eat our dal bhat, Aaron gives us a preview of the rest of the day. "Today we're meeting with a small group of pastors and church leaders here in this village. All of them have other jobs, and only a couple of them get any financial support for any work they do in the church."

"Are they coming from other villages?" Sigs asks.

"Yes, many of them have traveled a long way to be here, and we're going to spend time teaching them from the Word and training them in church planting." We soon find out that the "teaching" and "training" will be far more for us than it will be for them.

## A Transformed Life

Once full on dal bhat, we grab our Bibles and make our way toward what looks like a newly constructed small tin structure overlooking the village. Apparently, this is where the church meets in this village. Waiting inside is a group of about twenty people sitting in a circle, drinking tea, and talking. When we arrive, we join the circle too and begin sipping our tea.

Thus begins about twelve hours of praying, studying the Bible, encouraging, and being encouraged by one another late into the night. Over the course of these hours, I become acquainted with the most humble, kind, gentle, strong pastors and church leaders I've ever met.

On my right are Ram and Rasila. Ram used to be an alcoholic. "I was known as a very bad man in my village," he tells us. Rasila, Ram's wife, nods her head in agreement.

"He wasn't just bad in our village," Rasila adds, "but also in our home. He was not a loving husband. And he was not a loving father to our children. Many days he left us alone, because he was out drinking and doing other bad things. I would fix dinner for him, but often he wouldn't come home. Or when he came home, it was not good.

"Some days," Rasila elaborates, with tears of past pain welling in her eyes, "I wanted to kill myself. But then I would look into the eyes of my children and stop."

Ram picks the conversation back up. "But then one day someone shared the good news of Jesus with me. I heard how I could have a new life through believing in Jesus, being forgiven of my sin, and having a relationship with God. I heard how I could be the man and husband and dad that I am supposed to be."

"He came home one day," Rasila shares, "and I was so surprised. He wasn't drunk, yet he was talking in a way that seemed crazy to me. He told us he wanted to become a Christian and he wanted us to become Christians together."

"What did you think about that?" I ask.

"I wanted to know what was making such a difference in my husband. He was acting so different, and he was talking about how he wanted to love and care for and provide for us better. So I was glad to learn more about Jesus, and eventually my children and I all decided to follow him. Today Ram is the most loving husband and father I could imagine," Rasila says, beaming. "I believe I am the luckiest woman in the world, and the luckiest wife, for sure."

"Who shared the gospel with you?" I ask Ram. He smiles and points across the circle to another couple.

## Up in Flames

Sitting on the other side of the circle is another couple, Seojun and his wife, Jin. I can tell that Seojun and Jin are not originally from these mountains, and I ask them how long they have lived here.

"About ten years," Seojun says. "Jin and I moved here from another country. We wanted to share the gospel and set up work to help amid poverty and disease. When we arrived in this country, we decided we didn't want to stay in the city. We wanted to move into the mountains to be as close as possible to people who were in need, so we built a home up here attached to a place where we could do ministry to people's needs. And one day I met Ram, and soon thereafter we met Rasila."

"So you've lived here ever since then?" I ask.

"Not exactly," Seojun answers.

Jin chimes in, "One night we heard noises at the door of our house and we could tell something was wrong. As we walked toward the door, we looked outside through the window and saw men holding guns and torches. All of a sudden the men started breaking the windows, and I screamed. I've never been so afraid."

"They yelled for us to leave," Seojun says, "and as we ran out the door, they set our house and the attached building on fire. Then they pointed their guns at us and shouted, 'Don't ever come back! You are not welcome in this village, and if you ever try to come back, we will kill you.'"

"I was so sad," Jin shares. "We really believed God had called us to work in that village, but we knew that if we stayed, we not only would be in danger ourselves but would also put people like

Ram and Rasila in danger. So the next morning, I prayed specifically for the men who had done this to our house, and then we left this village, moving on to another place. When that house and ministry building burned, I thought our work here had gone up in flames, as well."

"So how are you back here now?" I ask.

"Over the coming years," Seojun answers, "we stayed in touch with Ram and Rasila and a few other people who had followed Jesus and started a church here. They started sharing with us how more people were coming to faith in Jesus and how he was changing others' lives and families, and the village, in powerful ways."

"Then one day," Jin says, "we heard about a natural disaster in this village that had destroyed over a hundred homes. Ram and Rasila said they needed help, so we came. We mobilized volunteers and supplies, and by God's grace we were able to help rebuild over one hundred homes."

"Is that when you built the place we're sitting in now for the church to meet?" I ask.

"That's a good question," Seojun replies. "But you'll have to ask *him* about that one." Seojun points back across the circle at a man we learn is named Bishal.

## From the Ashes

Bishal looks older, rougher, and tougher than anyone else in the room, yet an innocent smile spreads across his face. That smile soon goes away, though, as he tells his story.

"I used to be a tribal militant," Bishal shares. "My job was to protect the villages around here from outside forces. That included protecting against Christians."

Knowing what I now know about the severe hostility against believers, I think, *This man must have some story.*

"I used to think Christians were spies who wanted to come into our villages and ruin our culture," Bishal continues. "So years ago, when some Christians were discovered, my commander told me to take my men and make it clear they needed to leave immediately or else they'd be killed. So one night, I gathered my men, we took our guns and some torches, and we went to their house."

My eyes shoot toward Seojun and Jin. I look back at Bishal. "You were the one banging on their front door that night?" I ask.

Bishal nods his head. "I put a gun in Seojun's face and told him to never come back. Then I burned down his house and the building next to it."

As I'm listening, I remember what Jin shared—that the next morning before they left, she and Seojun had prayed for the men who threatened their lives and burned their home. "For years, I kept other Christians out, and I tried to keep Ram and Rasila and others as contained and quiet as possible," Bishal says. "But then the natural disaster hit, and within a matter of days those Christians I had threatened were here wanting to help rebuild our homes! I didn't know what to think, but I didn't want to refuse their help. Over the next couple of months, they brought food and supplies to us, and together we rebuilt all the homes that had been destroyed."

Smiles now spread around the circle as Bishal shares, "That's when the real miracle happened and I became a follower of Jesus. And as soon as I did, I offered my land to house this building for the church to meet in."

Bishal looks at me and says, "It has not been easy. The other militants, including my commander, labeled me a traitor and I lost a lot of land. But it has been worth it. My life, my family, and this village have been transformed by God's love through these two couples in this room." He looks at Seojun and Jin across from him, then at Ram and Rasila next to him.

I am speechless. And I remain that way as Ram and Rasila share more about how they've not only planted a church here in this village but also sent missionaries to plant churches in other villages. They're now part of a network of churches in this region, sharing the gospel and planting new churches, even among people of different languages.

The work Seojun and Jin started didn't go up in flames after all.


## Hard Work

The leaders in this room are all from the network of churches in this area. As the day goes on, we hear stories about how God is working and what challenges the churches are facing.

A woman named Nisu shares how she and her husband have planted a church in a remote village where the people have no written language. So they started working with villagers on creating a script and written language for their people. Many were excited about it, but not long after the project started, one of the village leaders gathered the villagers and said, "The only reason these Christians want to establish our language in writing is so they can translate the Bible, and we don't want the Bible, so this must stop."

Enough people were convinced that having a written language would be bad, so now the villagers are working to stop creation of their language in writing.

A man named Sai shares how the church he pastors has been trying to plant a church in one particular village for the last ten years but that every time someone starts to express interest in the gospel, something bad seems to happen in the village. As he shares his story of one failed attempt after another, Aaron leans over and whispers, "This is why many people who move here don't make it. This is hard work, and it doesn't succeed overnight. What's needed are people who are willing to work hard for ten or twenty years until a breakthrough happens. But a lot of Christians, and most churches in America who send them, aren't willing to stick it out that long."

I know he's right, which is troubling. I wonder if I would be willing to stick it out myself.

Finally, a man named Bibek shares about dire physical needs in the place where he is pastoring. His village is so remote that basic supplies are extremely hard to come by, and until he got there, no one in the village had heard the gospel. Now there's a small church that meets, and the members care for one another, and he just wants to learn how to best love and lead them.

"How remote is your village?" I ask.

"Very remote," Bibek responds as others in the room smile.

"Ask him how long it took him to get here from his village for this meeting," Ram says to me.

"How long did it take you?" I ask.

"About three weeks."

## The Church as God Designed It

So what do I say to church leaders who've traveled (at least some of them) for weeks to gather together? I'm humbled by the challenge—and opportunity. Aaron had asked me to spend the afternoon and evening teaching on what God's Word says about the church. So that's what I do.

Over the coming hours, we walk through all kinds of pictures and passages in the Bible describing the church as God designed it. As I'm teaching and we're all discussing what we see in God's Word, I am struck with two fresh realizations.

First, looking at the Bible to see how God has designed the church is exactly what needs to be done. As I had reflected a couple of days ago, these villages need the church in them, but they don't need an American version of church; they need a biblical version of church.

As I walk through the Word with these leaders, it hits me that so many of my conversations about the church in America are often focused on cultural traditions that are extrabiblical at best and unbiblical at worst.

For example, as I read the Bible with these brothers and sisters, we don't see anything about constructing church buildings or organizing church programs or managing church staffs, topics that so many church conversations in America revolve around. It makes me wonder, *Why are Bible-believing, Bible-preaching churches in America so focused on what is not in the Bible?* As I ask myself this question, I can't help but think that one of the greatest needs not just in the church in the Himalayas but in the place where I live is for us to open up our Bibles with fresh, unfiltered eyes and ask, "Are we really doing church the way this Book describes it?"

This leads to a second realization, which takes me back to Luke 14. If being a Christian means counting the cost and laying down your life, your possessions, your plans, and your dreams to follow Jesus wherever and however he leads you, then being a church means gathering together with people who have counted that cost and who are laying down their lives in this way. Which is exactly what I see around this room.

Not one person here is under the illusion that following Christ is easy. Not one person is here because it's culturally acceptable to be a Christian, and not one person is here because this is the most comfortable way for him or her to live.

Every person I'm speaking to is in this room because he or she wants to follow Jesus totally, knowing that means making sacrifices, doing hard things, and going into difficult (even dangerous) situations to spread God's love. And with our Bibles open, I am reminded that, well, this is what God designed the church to be.

It's after midnight by the time I get to my sleeping bag. I'm physically exhausted, yet spiritually exhilarated. Before my eyes shut, I write the following:

*After time with Alisha, Ram, Rasila, Seojun, Jin, Bishal, Nisu, and Bibek, I am all the more convinced the church can change the world. If we do church right. According to God's Word. Not according to our ways, ideas, trends, and traditions. If we count the cost as Christians and we become the church God has called us to be.*

## Reflections

What is it costing you to follow Jesus in your life right now? What steps of obedience to Jesus might make following him costlier?

Why do you think so many Bible-believing, Bible-preaching churches in America are so focused on what is not in the Bible? How could you be part of changing that?

# Day 7: Broken Teacups Shining Light

## Seeking the One

Today is the last day of the trek. Aaron told us that as we reached a lower altitude, it would get warmer, and indeed it has. I slept with my sleeping bag open the entire night, and I don't even think I'll need a jacket today. It's amazing what a difference a few thousand feet makes in the mountains.

I open up my Bible and turn again to Luke.

All the tax collectors and sinners were approaching
to listen to him. And the Pharisees and scribes were

complaining, "This man welcomes sinners and eats with them."

So he told them this parable: "What man among you, who has a hundred sheep and loses one of them, does not leave the ninety-nine in the open field and go after the lost one until he finds it? When he has found it, he joyfully puts it on his shoulders, and coming home, he calls his friends and neighbors together, saying to them, 'Rejoice with me, because I have found my lost sheep!' I tell you, in the same way, there will be more joy in heaven over one sinner who repents than over ninety-nine righteous people who don't need repentance.

"Or what woman who has ten silver coins, if she loses one coin, does not light a lamp, sweep the house, and search carefully until she finds it? When she finds it, she calls her friends and neighbors together, saying, 'Rejoice with me, because I have found the silver coin I lost!' I tell you, in the same way, there is joy in the presence of God's angels over one sinner who repents."

He also said: "A man had two sons. The younger of them said to his father, 'Father, give me the share of the estate I have coming to me.' So he distributed the assets to them. Not many days later, the younger son gathered together all he had and traveled to a distant country, where he squandered his estate in foolish living. After he had spent everything, a severe famine struck that country, and he had nothing. Then he went to work for one of the citizens of that country, who sent him into his fields to feed pigs. He longed to eat his fill from the pods that the pigs were eating, but no one would give him anything. When he came to his senses, he said, 'How many of my father's hired workers have more than enough food, and here I am dying of hunger! I'll get up, go to my father, and say to him, "Father, I have sinned against heaven and in your sight. I'm no longer worthy to be called your son. Make me like one of your hired workers."' So he got up and went to his father. But while the son was still a long way off, his father saw him and was filled with compassion. He ran, threw his arms around his neck, and kissed him. The son said to him, 'Father, I have sinned against heaven and in your sight. I'm no longer worthy to be called your son.'

"But the father told his servants, 'Quick! Bring out the best robe and put it on him; put a ring on his finger and sandals on his feet. Then bring the fattened calf and slaughter it, and let's celebrate with a feast, because this son of mine was dead and is alive again; he was lost and is found!' So they began to celebrate.

"Now his older son was in the field; as he came near the house, he heard music and dancing. So he summoned one of the servants, questioning what these things meant. 'Your brother is here,' he told him, 'and your father has slaughtered the fattened calf because he has him back safe and sound.'

"Then he became angry and didn't want to go in. So his father came out and pleaded with him. But he replied to his father, 'Look, I have been slaving many years for you, and I have never disobeyed your orders, yet you never gave me a goat so that I could celebrate with my friends. But when this son of yours came, who has devoured your assets with prostitutes, you slaughtered the fattened calf for him.'

" 'Son,' he said to him, 'you are always with me, and everything I have is yours. But we had to celebrate and rejoice, because this brother of yours was dead and is alive again; he was lost and is found.' " (15:1–32)

As I read these three stories, I am struck by the common themes in all of them. Each story is focused on the one. The first story is about one sheep out of a hundred. The second is about one coin out of ten. The third is about one son (although the second son clearly ties into the meaning of that story as well). In each story, the one is first lost and then found. And in each story, there's exuberant joy and celebration when the one is found.

The collective meaning of all three stories, then, is clear: God is passionate about finding the one, which is remarkable when you think about it. God has a universe to run, galaxies to uphold, governments to rule, and more than seven billion people to sustain, yet the Bible doesn't say that heaven rejoices over these cosmic mysteries and universal realities. Instead, something special happens in heaven when one person who was separated from God in sin is restored to God in love.

As I read, I see myself in the one, and I'm overwhelmed by God's grace. I journal,

*Lord God, my Father in heaven, thank you for seeking after me! Thank you for finding me! Thank you for finding my lost and sinful soul. Thank you for making me your son!*

But I can't stop there, not after what I've seen this week. I think of the individuals I have met: Kamal. Sijan and his baby boy, Amir. That precious girl who first held my hand, then spit at me. The mom, the dad, and the three-year-old daughter who hosted us for tea. Each man and woman mourning over burning bodies. Each child laughing and playing in the school we visited. The faithful pastors. God doesn't just love the crowds—he loves the one. And I want to be a reflection of him in my life. I write,

*O God, make my life a reflection of your seeking love. You seek the lost. You leave the many in search of the one. O God, I want my life to illustrate this. O God, please show yourself as the seeking and saving and loving and for- giving Father through me and my family and my church. Help me to care for the one right around me, and help me to leave and go to the one wherever you might lead me. Where I live. Here in the Himalayas. Wherever you lead me.*

As I write these words, I have no idea what God is getting ready to teach me about the importance of the one.

## Not Just a Number

I roll up my sleeping bag and stuff it into my pack one last time (at least for this trek). It's hard to believe that only one week has gone by because I feel I've experienced a year's worth of encounters the last few days.

As I'm packing, I hear a commotion outside. A female voice, sounding panicked and out of breath, is asking for Aaron. I hear Aaron step out from his room. The rest of us follow.

"What's wrong, Niyana?" Aaron asks.

Niyana is one of the teachers at the school we visited two days ago. She had stayed in the village when we left yesterday morning but got up extremely early this morning to hurry down the mountain to catch us before we left.

"I have horrible news," she says.

By this time, Alisha, who also teaches at the school, has come out of her room and is standing by Niyana.

"You know Pradip," Niyana says, looking toward Alisha.

Alisha nods and then turns to Aaron and says, "He's one of the five-year-olds in the school." She turns back to Niyana and asks, "What happened?"

"He was at school a couple of days ago, playing with all the other kids who were there," Niyana explains. She turns and says to us, "You all would have seen him. He was feeling fine, maybe a little tired but totally attentive and engaged at school. But then he went home not feeling well. That night he had diarrhea and started vomiting. His parents kept him home from school the next day, yet we didn't know anything was wrong. Apparently, Pradip kept getting worse and worse, and late last night, he died." Tears roll down Niyana's cheeks.

Shock spreads across Alisha's face, and her tears flow too.

"Alisha," Niyana says, "I knew you would want to know as soon as possible so you could go and be with Pradip's family."

We learn soon that Alisha was particularly close to Pradip and had formed a strong relationship with his family.

"Yes," Alisha says, wiping away her tears. "I'll get my stuff and walk back up with you right away." With that she enters her room. The door closes and we hear weeping.

We all stand quietly. Aaron says softly, "Niyana, why don't you and I think about some things we can do for Pradip's family." She nods her head, and together they step to the side to talk.

The rest of us turn around and walk silently back to our rooms to finish packing. As I stand over my bag, I picture the kids we played with just two days ago. Despite all the hardship I had seen and heard about in these mountains, the thought never occurred to me that within thirty-six hours, one of those kids could die from a surge of disease. Sure, I'd heard Aaron tell the statistics about half the children here dying before their eighth birthday. But somehow that phrase "half the children" had remained ambiguous to me. It was general and hard to imagine. But now I don't just have a number. I have a name: Pradip.

Kind of like Isaiah, my five-year-old back home.

It's easier to stomach poverty as long as you just look at numbers on a page. The poor are easier to ignore if they're a statistic.

But everything changes when you know one of them. Everything changes when you spend time with one and then two days later he's dead.

Not only does he die, but he's dead because he was poor.

If Isaiah has diarrhea and is vomiting, I have an easy fix. Give him plenty of clean water to drink. Give him some simple medicine to swallow. And if that doesn't work, I can drive him anytime day or night to a doctor or hospital to get him care. It would never even cross my mind that such an illness could be fatal. Such is the fruit not just of wealth but of privilege in this world, for even most of the poor in my country have access to basic medical care.

I sit on my bed and ask myself, *So what should I do with the wealth and privilege I have?* Ignorance of the poor and of the opportunities I have to help the poor is no longer possible. Neither is indifference. I know Proverbs 21:13, and it couldn't be any clearer: "The one who shuts his ears to the cry of the poor will himself also call out and not be answered." And based on what I read in Luke 15 this morning, "the poor" aren't just a general, ambiguous group of statistics. They're people. They're children like Pradip.

And God's response to me will be a reflection of my response to individuals like Pradip. That's a humbling thought (frightening, really) for me—and all Christians who possess any measure of wealth and privilege.

So how should I live? I don't suppose I can change the healthcare system for multitudes of people in this part of the world. But surely there's a way I can care for one of these kids. Surely there's a way I can care for one of these families. In light of Luke 15, the least I can do is love *one*.

But even that's not easy, as I find out a few minutes later.

## Chair on the Trail

Breakfast is quiet as the reality of this morning's news sets in. Alisha and Niyana grab a quick bite before we pray for them. Then they head back up the trail.

Even Aaron is now silent. He has loved and served these people for many years, but he's not grown numb to a tragedy like this. As we finish eating, Aaron tells us today's plan: "We have a short hike this morning that will lead us to a trailhead where we'll catch a bus and ride back into the city. Eat some snacks as you walk," he advises us, "because you don't want to get on that bus with an empty stomach. If you haven't eaten, these roads winding up, down, around, and through the mountains will not be your friend."

Promptly, we all pull out the last snacks and bars we brought with us and place them in our pockets. We hoist our packs over our shoulders, and as we start to hike, I admit to myself, *I'll be glad tomorrow to walk without this pack on my back.*

Before long, I see Chris, Sigs, and Aaron stopped ahead talking to some men. One of them is sitting in a chair on the trail, which is odd. As I get closer, I hear Aaron talking, and I can't believe what I'm hearing—and seeing!

One of the men is explaining how Kush, the man in the chair, lives in the village of the church where we worshipped a few days ago. The two men with Kush are part of the church. Apparently, one day recently, after working in the fields, Kush was walking home, when a large rock tumbled down the mountain toward him on the trail. He jumped to get out of the way and fell way down the mountain slope, breaking at least one of his legs (he has extreme pain in both). Some villagers found him and helped pull him back up on the trail. However, Kush couldn't walk, and he still can't. He needs significant medical attention fast, but obviously such assistance is nowhere nearby.

Church members heard about Kush's problem and offered to help him get down the mountain to a hospital, so two men found a wooden chair and some rope. They sat Kush in the chair and fastened him to it. Then they made two straps for the chair to go on someone's shoulders, much like a backpack. As they're explaining this, I look at this man fastened to a chair with ropes. *There's no way this is working,* I think. But, sure enough, it is.

After Aaron and all the men converse some more, one of the men squats down and swings his arms through the rope straps. The second man leans Kush and his chair toward the back of the first man, who now stands, hunched over, with a 150-pound man on his back. And then the first man starts walking down the trail—with Kush on his back!

I hope by now you have at least some sense of how challenging it is to walk these trails with a simple twenty-pound pack on your back, which, by the way, is ergonomically designed for a hiker's comfort. Such trekking is complicated only by ledges that are high, steep, and narrow, in addition to rocks of all sizes to step over and around and tree branches that threaten to catch you.

For all these reasons, it is mesmerizing to see this man carry Kush in a chair on his back. Apparently, the two men have alternated carrying Kush over the last couple of days. They, too, are planning to catch a bus at the trailhead, where they will ride with Kush to a hospital.

I think I'm seeing in person what I read about in Luke 5, just days earlier, how a paralytic man's friends carried him to Jesus. And as I walk behind a man carrying another man on his back, my pack suddenly feels lighter.

Further, as I reflect on what I read in Luke 15 this morning, I realize that, indeed, caring for the one is not always as easy as it might sound.

## One Is Found

While we hike, as Aaron forecast, the temperature rises, and soon I'm sweating. Six days ago, I was so cold I couldn't imagine ever sweating again. Now I start shedding layers for the final leg of the trek.

The scenery is different too. When we began six days ago, all the terrain was white. Now lush greens and bright browns color the landscape. It's beautiful in an entirely new way. We're following the river, walking back and forth across it on suspended steel bridges. The floors of the bridges are grated, so you can see the water rushing over rapids far below. Some bridges are sturdier than others, and some of them shake and sway when a strong wind gust hits. It's a bit nerve racking when that happens, and you move across as quickly as you can.

As I walk, I start to reminisce about the week. I wonder how I'm going to summarize for Heather and the kids all I've experienced. I feel as if any attempt to describe it all will be woefully inadequate. Still, I can't wait to see them and give it a try.

But there are more experiences still to come. As we approach the trailhead, Aaron tells us that before we board the bus, we will stop quickly at two places. The first is a center for children with disabilities. Specifically, we're going to meet a teenager named Malkit.

Malkit, we soon learn, has cerebral palsy, which affects his muscle coordination, vision, hearing, speech, and ability to swallow food. Malkit was born in one of the villages we walked through this week. When Malkit was ten years old, Nabin discovered him chained in a barn.

Malkit's family thought he was cursed and didn't know how to care for him, so he grew up with the animals in the barn. When Nabin found him, Malkit didn't know how to walk. Nabin, having been chained in a barn once himself, immediately began working to rescue Malkit. With the support of Malkit's family, Nabin and Aaron brought him down the mountain and, along with many others, they shared God's love with him. Not long ago, they helped him settle in at this center, where he has care for his unique needs.

As we walk in, Malkit sees Aaron and Nabin, and a contagious smile sweeps his face. He's full of joy as he walks over (yes, he's walking now!) to Aaron and Nabin and gives them both huge hugs. Malkit starts saying through slurred speech how thankful he is for how these men shared and showed God's love to him. He also says how much he enjoys living at this center, the friends he has, and all the things he's able to do, including physical therapy and all kinds of group activities and games.

I smile as I watch Aaron and Nabin interact with Malkit. Here's a young man who once was chained in a barn, living with animals, unable to walk, with no one to help him. Now he's smiling and walking and playing and hugging and laughing. And, best of all, he knows that God loves him enough to send Jesus to make it possible for him to have eternal life.

There's a lot to celebrate when, in a Luke 15 way, one who was lost has been found.

## Rescued by Love

Our visit at the center is short, and we quickly make our way to the second stop.

"This is a home for girls who were trafficked from these villages," Aaron says. "They were rescued from brothels and brought here for schooling and job training. And here they learn about the God who gives them hope for their future."

With this setup, we walk into the facility. I am floored.

I look around a room and see the faces of girls who look so young. They appear to be twelve to fourteen, maybe as old as sixteen, but hardly much older than that. As I look at their faces, just children really, and think about what they've been through, I have to look away before I lose my composure.

On a table in the room, I see cracked glass teacups. The woman who leads the home, Liv, tells us how these cups were an art project. In a recent class, the group talked about seeing beauty in the middle of brokenness. Each girl was given a glass teacup and asked to break it by throwing it on the floor. The girls were hesitant at first, but one by one they threw their cups and watched them shatter into pieces. Then each girl was asked to glue her cup back together, piece by piece.

Next they placed a small candle inside each cup and lit it. The cracks in those broken cups actually allowed the light of the candles to shine brighter. That led to a discussion of how in our lives we might feel broken because of what we've done or what's been done to us. But if we let him, God puts us back together and the light of his love shines brightly for others to see, even through our hurts.

Now, Liv tells us, the girls have just put the finishing touches on a painting. I look back around the room and see them laughing and smiling with pride over what they've created together. It's a painting of the world on a light-blue and white canvas. A diverse array of blended watercolors fills the continents and countries on the map. In the middle stands a Bible verse written in bold, ornate black letters. "Let the peoples praise you, O God; let all the peoples praise you!" (Psalm 67:3, ESV). Indeed, I think, there's much to celebrate when those who were lost (even enslaved in the horrors of sex trafficking) are found and rescued by the love of God.

## Breakdown

Aaron tells us we need to catch our bus, so we leave the home and make our way quickly toward the bus stop. We climb the stairs into a bus with bench seats similar to those on the bus I rode to elementary school.

Sitting down, my heart is about to burst with emotion after what I just saw at the home for girls, but, unfortunately, the next six hours are not conducive to reflection. While seeing a man carry another on his back as he crisscrossed over the river, visiting the center for disabled children, and then going to the home for freed girls, I totally forgot to eat anything. So when the bus rumbles off, I realize, *This is not going to be pleasant.* And, indeed, it's not.

Hour after hour we slowly wind down the mountain on narrow roads. At numerous points the road is only wide enough for one vehicle, so when we meet another driver, we stop and wait to ensure that one of the vehicles doesn't roll off the side. The farther we descend, the faster the bus goes, which means we're getting to our destination more quickly. However, that also means the bus is careening, sliding us around in our seats. I feel carsick but, along with others, try to sleep in order to pass the time.

By the time we arrive at the main bus stop in the city, it's already nighttime. We disembark in the darkness with our packs and walk toward the guesthouse where we're staying. We're exhausted, ready to crawl into a bed and sleep.

But as we walk through the streets with shops and restaurants on both sides, I notice that this scene reminds me of something I heard about in the mountains. On my left is a normal-looking clothing shop. Right next to it, I see what looks like a restaurant, but each of the booths here is walled in on all sides and has a door. As my gaze widens, I see two young girls sitting at the entranceway of the restaurant with blank looks on their faces. They're about the same age as the girls I saw this morning in the home near the trailhead. Immediately, it hits me: I'm looking at a brothel.

I catch Aaron and ask, "Am I seeing what I think I'm seeing?"

"Yes. I didn't know if you'd notice."

Before this trip, I would not have known about what was happening on this street. I would have thought this looked like a family-friendly part of town, where people shop and grab something to eat. But now my eyes see something totally different.

My jaw drops as we walk and I look around me. I see a couple of shops, and then a cabin restaurant with more girls out front. Then two more shops and another cabin restaurant. Then another. Then another. We round a corner and I see another. We cross over to a different street entirely—there's another.

Young girls sit in front of every restaurant. I look into one of their faces. She looks at me and smiles. Then she motions for me to come to her. I look away in horror. I feel filthy that she would even assume I want to use and abuse her. In a tense twist of emotions, I want to run from her and rescue her at the same time.

As we continue walking, I get to the point where I can hardly look at anything around me. I just don't want to see any more of this. I don't want to see these cubicles in restaurants and imagine what is happening inside them. I don't want to see the faces of girls for whom being trafficked for sex is their way of life. As we walk, I just want to look at my feet and pretend none of this is real.

Finally, we round the last corner and arrive at the guesthouse. Aaron gives instructions about picking us up in the morning for the ride to the airport, but I have trouble listening. I continue to look at my feet. My mind is racing. As soon as he finishes, I walk to my room without a word. I close the door, take off my pack, and fall on my face.

That's when it happens. I start to sob. Uncontrollably. I weep. And I can't stop.

"Why, God?" I cry out. "I don't understand why! Why do you let little girls suffer that? Why do you let men be that evil? Please make it stop! Like now, God, please make it stop *now*! Please strike down those men. Please, O God, save those girls . . . please save them! Why don't you save them—right now?"

I keep weeping. And I don't get it. I don't think I'm righteous. I know I'm a sinner. And I know God is righteous. And I know God is just. But I don't understand how what I've seen reconciles with the righteousness and justice of a loving God.

And it's not just what I've seen walking by those cabin restaurants. It's what I've seen throughout the mountains the last week. All their faces flood my mind as my face is on the floor. I see the cavity in Kamal's face. I see the spit on the young girl's chin. I see kids who might die tomorrow of diarrhea. I see more bodies on funeral pyres. And amid such massive physical suffering on earth, few of these people have ever heard how they can go to heaven.

"I just don't get it, God!" I cry. "Why, why, why?"

"Or what?" I ask. "I don't want to just question you, God, so what are you telling me to do? You love every one of these people, including every one of these girls! I prayed this morning that I would be a reflection of your searching love, so what does that mean?"

At this point I stand up and think, *Should I just go back out on the streets and pull these girls from these restaurants?* But as soon as I ask the question, I know the realities. I have no clue where I would take them. I can't even speak their language. And I remember how Aaron explained that the police are corrupt and actually part of the trafficking scheme, so I would be signing up for my own arrest.

*I don't want to make excuses, and I want to do something, but I don't know what to do.*

I fall face first again, this time on the bed, as I confess through tears, "O God, I have so many questions. There is so much I don't understand."

After a long pause, I continue. "But I'm going to trust that you hate evil far more than I do. And I'm going to trust that you love people in need far more than I do. So I'm offering you my life, in a fresh way, right now. Use me, O God, however you want to use me to make your Luke 15–like love known to the one. To the one man, woman, boy, or girl in a world of urgent spiritual and physical need."

As I lie on that bed thinking about the different "ones" I've seen over the last week, in light of Luke 15 I realize something: *There's really only one thing worse than being lost. What's worse is being lost when no one is trying to find you.*

With that thought, my face in the pillow, I fall asleep thinking about the individual ones I've encountered who, at that moment, have no one trying to find them.

## Reflections

Picture yourself in that guesthouse at the end of this trek. How would you summarize the thoughts in your mind? How would you summarize the emotions in your heart?

How would you pray as an expression of these thoughts and emotions?

# Day 8: Something Needs to Change

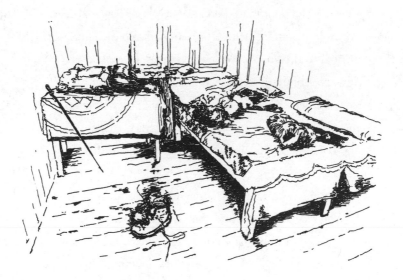

## The Stakes Are High

I wake up with sunlight creeping through the window. I'm still in my clothes from the trek but remember that I left a fresh set here for the flight home. After cleaning up, I put the clean clothes on and feel (and, honestly, look and smell) like a new person.

Aaron will come soon to pick us up for the trip to the airport. I open my Bible and journal for a few minutes alone with God:

There was a rich man who would dress in purple and fine linen, feasting lavishly every day. But a poor man named

Lazarus, covered with sores, was lying at his gate. He longed to be filled with what fell from the rich man's table, but instead the dogs would come and lick his sores. One day the poor man died and was carried away by the angels to Abraham's side. The rich man also died and was buried. And being in torment in Hades, he looked up and saw Abraham a long way off, with Lazarus at his side. 'Father Abraham!' he called out. "Have mercy on me and send Lazarus to dip the tip of his finger in water and cool my tongue, because I am in agony in this flame!"

"Son," Abraham said, "remember that during your life you received your good things, just as Lazarus received bad things, but now he is comforted here, while you are in agony. Besides all this, a great chasm has been fixed between us and you, so that those who want to pass over from here to you cannot; neither can those from there cross over to us."

"Father," he said, "then I beg you to send him to my father's house—because I have five brothers—to warn them, so they won't also come to this place of torment."

But Abraham said, "They have Moses and the prophets; they should listen to them."

"No, father Abraham," he said. "But if someone from the dead goes to them, they will repent."

But he told him, "If they don't listen to Moses and the prophets, they will not be persuaded if someone rises from the dead." (Luke 16:19–31)

What a story to read after the last week. The contrast in the passage is clear: On one hand, God responds to the needs of the poor with compassion. This is the only parable Jesus tells where someone is named, so why "Lazarus"? The answer is because his name means "one whom God helps." Lazarus is obviously poor—sick, crippled, laid at the gates of the rich, where he eats scraps while dogs feed on his sores. Yet God is committed to helping him.

In all of Scripture, not just this parable, God hears the cries of the poor and needy (Job 34:28). He satisfies them (Psalm 22:26), rescues them (35:10), provides for them (68:10), defends their rights (82:3), raises them up (113:7), and upholds their cause with justice (140:12). Clearly, God is the helper of the poor, the One who responds to their needs with compassion.

On the other hand, God responds with condemnation to those who neglect the poor. This rich man is not in hell because he had wealth; instead, he is in hell because he is a sinner whose heart indulged in his own luxuries while he ignored the poor. Actually, he threw scraps to them. He knew they existed, but he did little to help them.

And the consequences could not be any higher. This parable may be the most horrifying picture of hell in all of Scripture. And it comes straight from the mouth of Jesus. The details are graphic—a man in the anguish of flames. A place of torment separated by a fixed chasm that can never be crossed for all eternity.

Now, the Bible is clear that our eternal state depends on faith in Jesus, not on any works we might do in his name. However, the Bible is also clear that those who have true faith in Jesus will show it with their works, particularly on behalf of those in need

(Matthew 25:31–46; James 2:14–26). So rich people who neglect the poor inevitably reveal the hidden reality that they are ultimately not people of God.

I write in my journal,

*O God, I don't want to be like this rich man. How should I spend my money? How should I spend my life? What do you want me to do? Do I move my life and family here? Or do I do something else totally different?*

As I wrestle with these questions, I continue reading in Luke:

Will any one of you who has a servant plowing or keeping sheep say to him when he has come in from the field, "Come at once and recline at table"? Will he not rather say to him, "Prepare supper for me, and dress properly, and serve me while I eat and drink, and afterward you will eat and drink"? Does he thank the servant because he did what was commanded? So you also, when you have done all that you were commanded, say, "We are unworthy servants; we have only done what was our duty." (17:7–10, ESV)

As soon as I read this passage, I fall on my knees and begin to journal through prayer in light of verse 10,

*O God, I am a servant reporting for duty today. You are my master. I don't want to*

*call the shots in my life. I only want to do my
duty. O God, I only want to get to the end and
say, "I am an unworthy servant; I have only
done what was my duty."*

As I'm writing and praying, and before I finish reading this passage in Luke 17, there's a knock on my door. Aaron is standing there holding a packing tube that looks like it has a poster inside.

"Good morning," he says, and I reply in kind. "It's about time to go, but as you pack your things, I wanted to give this to you to put in your bag," he says, holding out the packing tube toward me.

"What is it?"

"Why don't you wait and open it later. Besides, we need to get going. Are you ready?"

"Sure," I say as I put the tube in my bag. Within minutes, I join the others, and after stowing our bags in the van, we head to the airport.

## Tired of Talking

Riding to the airport next to Aaron, who is driving, I ask, "Aaron, weren't you a pastor of a church before you moved out here?"

"I was."

"And that was after you had that first experience hiking, right?"

"Yeah. When I came back down the mountain after meeting that trafficker, I decided I was going to do everything I could to spread the gospel and show God's grace in these mountains. But I didn't immediately move out here. Instead, I served as a pastor, mobilizing people for work here. Along the way I started building a team—with people from this country as well as from churches in other countries."

"That's interesting," I say as I think about my own desire as a pastor to mobilize people for work in different places around the world. "So what made you decide to leave pastoring a church in order to move your family here?"

Aaron smiles and pauses. I can tell he's hesitant to answer, almost like he doesn't want to say what he's thinking. So I ask again, "Why'd you do it?"

"Do you really want to know?"

"I've asked you twice now." I laugh as I say it. "Yes, I really want to know!"

"I got tired of talking." He smiles.

Now I understand why he was hesitant to answer. Aaron didn't want to offend me. I am a pastor . . . who does a lot of talking.

"I felt like I was *talking* about ministry in the midst of urgent spiritual and physical need," Aaron says, "more than I was *doing* ministry in the midst of such needs. And I decided *that* needed to change."

## Living with Urgency

With that, we arrive at the airport. Aaron gives us instructions on how to navigate the ticket counter and immigration in order to get to our flight on time. As he shakes hands with each of us, I realize that over the course of an unforgettable week, he has become a good friend.

"Thank you, Aaron, for inviting me—and us—out here," I tell him. Since I'm wondering if I might move here one day, I say, "I'm not sure yet how, but you can count on me—and us—being part of this work in the days ahead."

He smiles, we hug, and off we all go into the terminal.

After waiting in line after line, Chris, Sigs, and I finally make it to our gate. The airport is old and fairly run down. There aren't many places to walk around, so we each find a not-so-comfortable seat for a few minutes before we board. I pull out my Bible and journal to finish Luke 17. There I read these words from Jesus:

> He told the disciples: "The days are coming when you will long to see one of the days of the Son of Man, but you won't see it. They will say to you, 'See there!' or 'See here!' Don't follow or run after them. For as the lightning flashes from horizon to horizon and lights up the sky, so the Son of Man will be in his day. But first it is necessary that he suffer many things and be rejected by this generation.
>
> "Just as it was in the days of Noah, so it will be in the days of the Son of Man: People went on eating, drinking, marrying and giving in marriage until the day Noah boarded the ark, and the flood came and destroyed them all. It will be the same as it was in the days of Lot: People went on eating, drinking, buying, selling, planting, building. But on the day Lot left Sodom, fire and sulfur rained from heaven and destroyed them all. It will be like that on

the day the Son of Man is revealed. On that day, a man on the housetop, whose belongings are in the house, must not come down to get them. Likewise the man who is in the field must not turn back. Remember Lot's wife! Whoever tries to make his life secure will lose it, and whoever loses his life will preserve it. I tell you, on that night two will be in one bed; one will be taken and the other will be left. Two women will be grinding grain together; one will be taken and the other left." (verses 22–36)

The point of this passage is plain. Jesus is telling his disciples that his return will be sudden and surprising. It can happen at any moment. As I sit in the airport, I realize that Jesus could come back right now. Or he could come back an hour from now, when I'm on this plane. He could come back before I get home. This day could be my last. And that means I need to live with urgency today for what matters forever.

So I journal,

> Oh, the urgency here! This could be the day when Jesus returns. Or tomorrow. Or the next day. I do not have time to waste. O God, please help me not to waste today. I want to live with urgency as long as I have life.

Yet even as I write this, I realize the danger that lies ahead for me as I'm about to board the plane, for I know if I'm not careful,

I could go home and, instead of living with urgency, easily settle into complacency. But the Kamals and trafficked girls and people on the verge of being placed on funeral pyres don't need my complacency. They don't need me, and other Christians, living as if somebody somewhere will do something someday about their urgent spiritual and physical needs; they need me, and other Christians, living like this day could be their last.

Our plane is about to board. As I put my Bible and journal away, Chris asks, "David, how would you summarize your takeaway from this trip?"

I don't have to think long to respond. I know exactly what God has said to me through his Word during this trek.

"Something needs to change," I say. "In my life. In my family. In the church. I don't know exactly what that means, but I just know I cannot—and we cannot—continue with business as usual.

"Something needs to change *now*."

## Reflections

In your life, where are you more prone to "talk" rather than "act" in living out the gospel?

As we prepare to think about what needs to change, what are the biggest barriers to potential change happening in your life? What are the most significant obstacles to your living with urgency for those in need right around you, as well as around the world?

# What Now?

So what needs to change? I certainly don't presume to know the answer to that question for you. My primary aim in sharing this trek has been to bring you to the point—along with me—of asking the question. To the point where you feel, hopefully in a fresh way in your heart, the urgent needs around us in the world, and to where you believe, even with all the questions you or I might have, that Jesus is indeed the ultimate hope amid such needs. Further, I hope you realize that God has designed your life to count for the spread of his hope amid the most hopeless situations in the world.

One of the dangers of trips like this is that we can experience varied emotions, and maybe even make various commitments, but within weeks of returning, our lives look just like they did before we went. Obviously, this has been a book and not a trip, but I wonder if the same danger is in play. I really believe this book has missed the mark if your life ends up looking just like it did before you read it.

I have thought much about Proverbs 24:11–12 since I first encountered the Himalayas face to face. God says,

> Rescue those being taken off to death,
> and save those stumbling toward slaughter.
> If you say, "But we didn't know about this,"
> won't he who weighs hearts consider it?
> Won't he who protects your life know?
> Won't he repay a person according to his work?

These verses of Scripture make clear that God holds you and me accountable for what we know. I'm accountable for what I have seen in those mountains, and now that you've read this book, you're accountable as well. If you and I know that people are suffering both physically and spiritually like this, then we are accountable before God for what we do (or don't do) in response.

## My Journey

When I flew back to the United States, Heather and the kids greeted me at the airport and we headed home together. It was late at night, so we put the kids to bed, a humbling and touching moment for me in light of what I'd seen in children's lives over the past week. Meanwhile, Heather was begging me to tell her all the details of the trip. Because of the remoteness of those mountains, we had hardly communicated during the time I had been gone. That meant she didn't know anything about what I'd been wrestling through, including the possibility that we might move overseas.

I knew I would be tired and jet lagged from the flight, so my plan was to wait until the next morning to sit with Heather and share about all that had happened. I knew this would be a sensitive conversation, so I wanted to be fully rested.

But Heather would have none of it—she wanted the details now. So we lay in bed as I scrolled through my journal, sharing different stories. I was physically struggling to stay awake as she asked me questions. Then right as I got to the point where I'd written that God might be leading our family to move overseas, there was a long pause in our conversation. Of course, she was soaking in this news. Unfortunately, in the pause, I fell soundly asleep.

Picture the scene: I've just told my wife that we could be moving to the Himalayan mountains, and she's in total shock. Meanwhile, I've disappeared into comatose sleep, snoring away.

Needless to say, first thing the next morning, Heather woke me, saying, "We need to pick up where we left off last night!"

Almost immediately we began exploring the possibility of a move. At the same time, an international missions organization (called the International Mission Board, or IMB) approached me about becoming the leader of that organization. The IMB represents tens of thousands of churches that collectively pool their resources to financially support thousands of missionaries who serve around the world in countries least reached with the gospel. At first I didn't want to entertain conversation with the IMB, but then I had to at least ask myself, *Why would I be willing to consider moving overseas but not be willing to consider a position focused on leading and mobilizing multitudes of people overseas?*

Even still, in the middle of all this, I loved the people in the church I was pastoring at the time and couldn't imagine leaving them. So I fell on my face before the Lord, daily, and prayed, "God, I'll do whatever you want me to do with all you've given me."

Over months of fasting and praying like this alone, with Heather, and with the pastors at our church, God clearly and unmistakably led me to the IMB, where I would serve for the next four years.

Yet that prayer of surrender continued—on a regular basis. Now living in Richmond, Virginia, as the leader of the IMB, I accepted an invitation to teach God's Word in metro Washington, DC, at McLean Bible Church. Through a series of unforeseen circumstances and unexplainable events, God clearly and unmistakably led me to begin pastoring this church in this global city where so many nations are represented and from which so many people leave to work among the nations. Pastoring this church eventually necessitated stepping aside from my role in the IMB.

As a pastor, I am now dreaming, planning, and working with brothers and sisters in our church from more than one hundred different nations for the spread of gospel hope around the world, beginning in greater Washington, DC. In addition, I along with Chris (from the trek) and others have worked to create a global ministry and giving platform aimed at mobilizing resources in the church for the spread of the gospel amid the most urgent needs in the world. I am more exhilarated than ever before about the opportunities that exist right now for the spread of the gospel. In Aaron's words, the last thing I want to do as a pastor is *talk* about ministry in the midst of urgent need. I want to *do* that kind of ministry! And I'm still wondering if one day God will lead me on a one-way trip to another part of the world.

## Your Journey

The reason I share all this is not to suggest that your path will look like mine. Actually, the point is that it won't. God is not calling every person to lead a missions organization, pastor a church, or become a missionary in another country. He's certainly calling some of us to do these things, and I have prayed that God would use this book to call many people in these ways. But God's call is not just for the leader, pastor, or missionary. God's call is for every one of us. Whether you're a teacher or trout-poop expert, a business professional or stay-at-home parent, a student or retiree, God has created your life to count in a world of urgent need.

So don't underestimate the part God is calling you to play, starting right where you live. Realize that God has you where you are for a reason. You are not in your city or community by accident. You are in your job, your school, your neighborhood, or your apartment complex with the gifts, skills, abilities, and resources you possess by divine design. God has sovereignly given you unique opportunities for the spread of gospel hope in the world around you.

I don't know the most urgent spiritual and physical needs around you, but God does. So ask him, "Where are the poor, the oppressed, the orphaned, the enslaved, and ultimately the lost right around me?" Then realize God loves those men, women, and children so much that he has put you in close proximity to them. He wants the hope of Jesus to be spread, shared, and enjoyed among them through your life.

Then realize that the effect of your life could extend far beyond where you currently live. Open your eyes to opportunities you have to use your time, your money, and your talents to spread the gospel where it hasn't gone and to serve people who desperately need to see and feel God's love face to face.

Think back to the stories I shared on the trek of opportunities for students, professionals, and retirees to leverage their unique gifts, skills, and experiences for the spread of gospel hope amid urgent need in the world. Then think about your life. What unique ways can your life count for the spread of his love in the world?

## The Challenge

In light of urgent needs around us and vast opportunities before us, I want to conclude this book with a challenge. The aim of this challenge is to help you discern what needs to change in your life, your family, your church, or your future as a result of the journey we've taken. The challenge is fourfold, and I offer it to you even as I challenge myself in the exact same ways.

### Work Hard to Help Well Amid Earthly Suffering

Every word in this part of the challenge is important. I'll start at the end. When I use the term *earthly suffering,* I am referring primarily to all kinds of physical suffering people are experiencing in the world. In terms of our trek, think about Kamal with a missing eye and lack of access to medical help. Or think of villages where kids and their parents are dying of cholera because they lack clean water. Think of special-needs kids chained outside their homes, or precious young girls enslaved and sold for sex.

The world around us is filled with earthly suffering. In the city where I live and every place I travel in the world, I see all kinds of suffering. I recently returned from Thailand, where I worked alongside brothers and sisters in trafficking ministries. Not long thereafter, I was in apartments and homes in metro Washington, DC, where families are struggling with severe physical needs. I served in a ministry at our church for children (and families) with special needs. The next week, I found myself on a trip to Ethiopia and Uganda supporting work among orphans and refugees. Unfortunately, the opportunities to help amid earthly suffering are not hard to find—for any one of us wherever we live and work.

The danger, however, is that we can so easily turn a blind eye and deaf ear to these opportunities. If we're not careful, we can isolate ourselves from the most severe suffering around us. We can cocoon ourselves in our homes and even in our church buildings; occupy ourselves with the busyness of life, school, work, and play; and never engage ourselves in being the hands and feet of Christ to the neediest around us.

So let's *help well* amid earthly suffering. My intent in emphasizing *well* here is to recognize that if we're not careful, even in our attempts to *help* we can actually end up hurting those we're trying to help—just think about the examples I mentioned above.

There are family situations in some parts of the world where parents send their children to an orphanage because they don't have the financial ability to feed them. Could it be more helpful to explore poverty-alleviation solutions among those parents that would enable them to keep their children?

Likewise, the men and women I worked with in Thailand are exploring wiser ways not just to rescue one young girl who has been sold into slavery but to keep hundreds of girls like her from being sold into slavery in the first place. For the sake of these girls—or, similarly, boys and men like them sold into slavery in the fishing industry in Thailand—it is incumbent on us to help well.

And to *work hard* toward that end. If we want to make a difference with those in need around us, it won't be easy. This takes true commitment. If we're not careful, we can reach out to those in need with a short act of service or a quick handout, only to pat ourselves on the back and move on. This is not what the gospel requires. We celebrate and imitate a King who "did not come to be served, but to serve, and to give his life as a ransom for many"

(Matthew 20:28). He "humbled himself by becoming obedient to the point of death—even to death on a cross" (Philippians 2:8).

Consequently, let's not fool ourselves, thinking there are easy fixes to earthly suffering. I think about Aaron in the Himalayas. He has spent years addressing urgent need in those mountains. He has encountered setback after setback after setback, yet he has persevered, working hard to help well amid earthly suffering. Though we won't all work on the same scale as he has, let's all work with the same resolve.

So where and how can you work hard to help well amid earthly suffering? As you answer that question personally and practically, consider a second part of this challenge.

### Work Hardest to Keep People from Eternal Suffering

The contrast between *eternal* suffering and *earthly* suffering in this part of the challenge is deliberate. As is the contrast between *hardest* and *hard*.

Here I draw a distinction between the types of suffering that people experience in this world and the everlasting suffering that people without Christ will experience beyond this world. One involves varying types of destitution; the other involves the most extreme kind of destitution (that is, damnation). One lasts for a limited number of years; the other lasts forever.

This is without question the reality that is most difficult to believe and understand. But this is a reality the Bible does not leave you or me with an option to disbelieve or put aside. Therefore, it only makes sense to work "hardest" here.

I challenge you to work hardest at sharing the gospel. Work hardest at sharing the message of God's holiness; our sinfulness; Jesus's unique life, death, and resurrection; and the urgent need for people to trust in him as Savior and Lord for eternal life. The gospel is the greatest news in all the world, it meets the greatest need in all the world, and, as such, we must work hardest at making it known.

Working to provide clean water, medical clinics, care for orphans, rescue from slavery, and all sorts of other earthly suffering is extremely significant. Yet ministry that addresses eternal suffering is infinitely more important. As I hope you've seen, no water filter, food program, medical clinic, or slavery rescue operation will by itself get anyone into heaven. Over and above all these physical needs is the need for reconciliation with God, and that need can be met only when the gospel is proclaimed.

This in no way means that we restrict help amid earthly suffering to those who believe the gospel. On the contrary, we hope that help for earthly suffering will ultimately shine more light on the gospel. And we believe that when someone believes the gospel, the heart is transformed and the church is started, paving the way for all sorts of greater ministry to address earthly suffering.

That actually leads to the next part of the challenge, but before moving on, let me pause and point out what I hope is obvious. You have opportunities to meet the greatest need in the world right now. Today. You are surrounded by people who are separated from God and on the way to eternal suffering. And you have the antidote to this problem! So find someone today—even right now—and share the gospel with him or her. And commit your life to doing this every day where you live.

And wherever God leads. I hope that trekking through the Himalayas has opened your eyes in a fresh way to the reality that many people in the world have little to no knowledge of the gospel. Many have never even heard the name of Jesus. I urge you to consider what ways your life, your family, or your church can play a part in getting the gospel to them. Think about it this way: how would you want a person on the other side of the world to live if you were on a road leading to an eternal hell and no one had ever told you how you could go to heaven? Answer that question, and then live accordingly.

## Be the Church God Calls Us to Be

Christianity prioritizes community, and no Christian follows Jesus in isolation from others. So this third part of the challenge pertains to our lives in the churches we belong to. The purpose of a local church is to be a display of the love of Christ in a local community and to send members out for the spread of hope beyond that community. The picture really is pretty simple when you think about it.

As we've seen on the trails, though, we can easily complicate the church. We can fill our churches with all kinds of things that are not in the Bible. We can focus our churches on buildings that cater to our comforts and budgets with programs that prioritize our preferences. But this is not who God has called the church to be or what God has called the church to do.

So I challenge you, in the church of which you are a part, to open your Bible with fellow Christians and put everything in the church on the table. Ask God what is most important to him in a world of urgent spiritual and physical need right around you and all around the world. Then pray together, "God, we will do whatever you want us to do with all you've given us."

In offering this prayer together, say to God, "If that means selling our building, we will do it. If that means eliminating every program, we will do it. If that means totally rearranging our budget, we will do it. Because we want your gospel to spread more than we want our traditions to keep, and we want your hope to be known, experienced, and enjoyed in a needy world more than we want our comforts in the church."

I obviously don't know what God will lead your church to do in response to that prayer. As we pray this prayer in the church I have the privilege of pastoring, I don't yet know all that he's going to lead us to do. Thankfully, though, God has not left us in the dark concerning what he has told us to do. We recently walked through essential traits of a church according to the Bible, and they're fairly simple and straightforward:

- Preach his Word.
- Share the gospel.
- Pray fervently and frequently.
- Worship together.
- Give together.
- Love one another.
- Help one another grow in Christ.

- Commit our lives together to making disciples and multiplying churches among the nations, no matter what it costs us.*

I challenge you and the other Christians in your church to give yourselves wholly to these things, confident that the church can actually change the world—if we do the church right.

In a world of urgent need, be the church God calls us to be.

## Run the Race God Calls You to Run

The key word in the final part of this challenge is to *run*. I don't mean to diminish the repeated exhortations in God's Word for us to *walk* with him. And I don't mean to encourage an unsustainable pace that leads to burnout. I'm not challenging you to sprint. And, well, I'm not overly concerned that too many of us are working way too hard for the spread of gospel hope in the world.

So in an intentional way, I challenge you, as in Hebrews 12:1–3, to see a world of urgent need around you and not sit still, and not even walk, but run. Right now.

I think about reading that final passage in Luke 17 in the airport on the way home. Jesus is coming back, and it could be anytime. You are standing right now on the doorstep of eternity, and you are not guaranteed tomorrow. So run while you still have time *today*.

Live with a holy sense of urgency, as if today could be your last. Jonathan Edwards, a pastor God used to fuel a Great Awakening

---

* For more detailed information on this topic, see "12 Traits: Embracing God's Design for the Church," https://radical.net/book/12-traits-embracing-gods-design-for-the-church.

in the church, wrote in his resolutions that he would recite every day, "*Resolved,* To think much, on all occasions, of my own dying, and of the common circumstances which attend death."* David Brainerd, known for giving his life in sharing God's love among Native American tribes who had little knowledge of the gospel, said almost the same thing throughout the journal of his short life before he died at age twenty-nine. You might think, *That's depressing. Why would I live like that?*

Here's why. Because you and I need to remember that our homes and our health and our bank accounts and our vehicles and our jobs and our comforts in this life guarantee us nothing in this world. One day (and it could be today) they're all going to be gone, so we need to remind ourselves to live today for what lasts forever.

We need to run for our own sake, and we need to run for the sake of others. For Kamal's sake. For Sijan's sake. For the sake of more girls who were trafficked yesterday, and more bodies that are burning on funeral pyres today. For the sake of people like you and me who desperately need a hope they won't find anywhere else in this world.

And not just for their sake. Ultimately for his sake. For the glory of Jesus in a world where he wills to be known as the One who alone can save from sin, heal the deepest hurt, and give eternal life. In the words of Hebrews 12:2, fix your eyes on Jesus and follow him with single-minded focus. For Jesus's sake, let gospel

---

* S. E. Dwight, *The Life of President Edwards* (New York: G. & C. & H. Carvill, 1830), 68, www.google.it.ao/books?id=kDxTqrWsOq4C&pg=PA70&focus=viewport&dq=editions:ISBN0803974612&lr=&as_brr=0&output=html_text.

reality in your head fuel gospel fervency in your heart that leads to gospel urgency in your life.

## Let All the Peoples Praise You

As you take the challenge I have outlined above, I offer you this guarantee: the more you give your life spreading the love of Jesus in a world of urgent need, the more you will experience the joy of Jesus in your life. I promise you, there are few things more fulfilling than bringing hope to the hurting, becoming family to the forgotten, announcing freedom to the captive, and leading those on a road to eternal death to know eternal life.

I want to take you back to that final morning in Asia before we headed to the airport. If you'll remember, Aaron gave me a packing tube that looked like it might hold a poster. Well, it wasn't a poster; it was a picture.

As soon as I opened and unrolled it, I realized where it came from. The girls in the home near the trailhead, who had been rescued from trafficking, had just finished making it when we came to visit. I remember their faces, smiling and giggling with joy and pride over their painting. It's a picture of the world with this verse beautifully written over it:

> Let the peoples praise you, O God;
> let all the peoples praise you! (Psalm 67:3, ESV)

I now look at this picture hanging on the wall in the central room in my home. It is a constant reminder for me of the pain these girls once felt and the joy they now know. In addition, it is a continual call for me to weep for those who are still hurting and to do all I can to make my life, family, and church count for the spread of God's love among them.

So I close with this simple question for your reflection—and action: What something needs to change in your life to effect change with the hope of Jesus in a world of urgent spiritual and physical need?

# Discussion Questions

## Why the Tears? / Preparation

1. When was the last time you came face to face with someone whose need was so urgent that it affected you emotionally? Describe how you felt and how you handled the situation.
2. With so many people hurting—spiritually and physically—in the world around us, why do you think many of us have lost our capacity to weep?
3. As you begin this journey, what do you hope to learn about addressing the world's most urgent needs?
4. Confronting needs related to poverty, injustice, and human trafficking can be risky. How would you prepare for a journey like this?
5. How can the gospel of Jesus Christ offer hope to people on the other side of the world who are suffering in ways that you may never experience?

## Day 1: Arrival

1. Have you ever traveled to another country or encountered a culture that was very different from your own? If so, describe your initial reaction to what you experienced.

2. How would a journey like that change the way you pray before and during the trip?

3. Why do you think going to a place like the Himalayas requires us to be able to communicate the gospel clearly? What basic truths should we not assume people understand?

4. On Day 1, David journals about John the Baptist's message of repentance (Luke 3:1–18). How would you explain the concept of repentance to someone who had no knowledge of the Bible?

5. Is it arrogant to urge people from another culture who are not followers of Christ to repent of what they have always believed in order to follow him? Explain your answer.

## Day 2: A Long Way to Go Before Dark

1. Does it surprise you that there are places in the world with little or no access to the gospel? How might this reality change the way you think about the urgency of the church's mission?

2. How does the story of meeting Kamal (the man who was missing an eye) help us see the relationship between meeting spiritual needs and meeting physical ones?

3. The kinds of physical suffering identified in Day 2—cholera outbreaks, abuse, sex trafficking, and hunger—cause some people to question God's goodness. What truths from the Bible help you make sense of these kinds of experiences, including how you should respond?

4. In Luke 6:24–26, Jesus warns us of the dangers of relying on earthly riches. What does it mean to have an eternal perspective when it comes to earthly riches and physical suffering?

5. What are some practical ways you could respond to what you read about in Day 2? What might these responses cost you in terms of comfort and resources?

## Day 3: Body Breakers and Butter Tea

1. Do most of the people you know tend to be more passionate about meeting spiritual needs or physical needs? Why do you think that is?

2. In Day 3, David reflects on Jesus's encounters with a mother who had lost an only child, as well as a woman who was desperate for physical healing (Luke 7:11–17; 8:40–56). What do these encounters teach us about Jesus's compassion? What do they teach us about his power over death and disease?

3. How would you respond to someone who said, "All religions are essentially the same"?

4. Although we should not ignore physical needs, why is it more critical to address spiritual ones?

5. Why is it important for Christians to trust in God's wisdom, as revealed in the Bible, rather than in our own wisdom about what "seems" fair? How can trusting God's wisdom help us when it comes to a topic such as hell?

## Day 4: I Saw Tiny Lights Moving
## up the Mountain

1. Like the expert in the law who questioned Jesus (Luke 10:25–37), we often try to come up with reasons why we don't have to love certain people as ourselves. What are some specific ways you've seen this play out in your life?
2. Describe in your own words what it means to "love your neighbor as yourself" (verse 27). Why does this kind of costly, sacrificial love require a heart that has been transformed by God?
3. What are some practical ways you could apply the command to love your neighbor as yourself in your own neighborhood and community?
4. Would you describe your prayers as relentless and bold? If not, why do you think you've been reluctant to pray that way?
5. How is the church that you read about in Day 4 different from the churches you're familiar with? What might we learn from this church in terms of how we spend our time and resources?

## Day 5: Nurses, Teachers, and
## Trout-Poop Experts

1. David's Scripture reading in Day 4 deals with the foolishness of finding security in earthly riches, as well as the need to be faithful with what the Lord has given us (Luke 12:16–21, 42–48). In what ways are you tempted to live for

your own comfort rather than leveraging your life to make Christ known?

2. How did the stories of nurses, teachers, and trout-poop experts help you reimagine how God might use the skills, gifts, and opportunities he has given you?

3. We often think we have to choose between meeting spiritual and physical needs. Based on your reading for Day 5, why is this a false dichotomy?

4. In your own experience, how have you seen spiritual conversations result from meeting physical needs? How might you be more intentional about encouraging these conversations in the future?

5. We normally think of all we have to give up in order to follow Christ. Why is it also important to remember that we gain infinitely more than we could ever lose (Luke 12:32–34)? How does this eternal reward motivate you to spend your life making Christ known?

## Day 6: Like a King Preparing for War

1. Jesus urges his would-be followers to count the cost, and he says that they must be willing to forsake everything for his sake (Luke 14:25–35). What kinds of things might following Jesus cost someone?

2. What are some ways we have watered down and distorted Jesus's costly call to discipleship? Why is this misrepresentation so dangerous as we tell people the good news of the gospel?

3. Why is it so important for followers of Christ to recognize that the greatest challenges to the church's mission—making disciples of all nations (Matthew 28:19)—are spiritual rather than physical? How should this reality affect the way we carry out our mission?

4. It is common for people to claim that following Jesus will lead to health, wealth, and prosperity (what is sometimes called the prosperity gospel). How do the passages you read in Day 6, as well as the stories of Alisha and others, expose the prosperity gospel as false?

5. If you're not already a follower of Jesus, what is keeping you from following him? Talk to a trusted Christian friend or pastor about any questions you have.

## Day 7: Broken Teacups Shining Light

1. What has been your biggest takeaway from this journey so far? What has surprised you the most?

2. The parables Jesus tells in Luke 15:1–32 highlight the fact that God is not indifferent to people—despite their sin. He graciously and gladly seeks them out. How does this truth change the way you think about your own salvation? How might it change the way you approach sharing the gospel?

3. How do real-life stories of suffering and costly obedience help you see the massive needs of the world from a new perspective?

4. Have you ever experienced something that, like David,

caused you to cry out, "Why, God?" How have the truths of Scripture helped you process what you experienced and felt?

5. Who are some specific individuals you know who need to hear the good news of a God who seeks out and saves the lost? Make a list and be intentional about planning time to talk with them about the gospel.

## Day 8: Something Needs to Change

1. Scripture is clear that we cannot earn our salvation by caring for the poor or by any other good work that we do (Luke 18:9–14; Ephesians 2:8–9). So, what is Jesus trying to teach us in the story of the rich man and Lazarus (Luke 16:19–31) when it comes to earthly riches and caring for the poor?

2. What does your use of money and possessions say about your faith?

3. Based on what you've read in Day 8 (as well as the previous Days), has your view changed about how the church should spend its time, resources, and energy? If so, how?

4. In what ways does the reality of hell, as well as the sudden and surprising nature of Christ's return, affect the urgency of the church's mission?

5. What are some specific needs that you could pray for on a regular basis in order to maintain an eternal, God-centered perspective on the needs of the world? Make a list and plan to incorporate these needs into your regular prayer routine.

# What Now?

1. What needs have you been exposed to in this journey that you feel compelled to act on?
2. What's one specific way your job, training, and/or station in life—for example, stay-at-home parent, student, retiree, salesperson, and so on—might be leveraged for the sake of meeting urgent spiritual and physical needs around the world?
3. What's wrong with responding to this journey as an isolated individual rather than as a member of a local church? How do you plan to involve pastors, fellow church members, and trusted Christian friends in the decision-making process for how you might respond to what you've read?
4. Why should addressing eternal suffering be our top priority? How can you make sure that spreading the gospel remains a primary focus in your own life? How will you try to keep God's glory as the ultimate motivating factor in all you do?
5. Living with urgency will look different for each of us. As you reflect on this journey through the Himalayas, what's one thing that needs to change in your life?

# Acknowledgments

This book is the fruit of God's grace toward me through so many people in so many ways.

I am grateful to God for a meeting one day in the Atlanta airport with Sealy, Curtis, Chris, and Lukas that led to this book almost three years later. Thank you, brothers, for your wise counsel, continual support, and personal encouragement.

I am grateful to God for Tina and the entire team at Multnomah, and particularly for Bruce and Dave. You have been patient with me and helpful to me in ways I desperately needed and didn't deserve. Thank you not only for taking this project on so graciously but, more importantly, for believing in it so strongly.

I am grateful to God for friends who have traveled with me to trek these trails, and especially for Tim, whose immense contributions got this book off the ground. Here's to long days, cold nights, challenging conversations, altitude sickness, broken bones, sore knees, stinging nettles, glacier avalanches, perpetual dal bhat, and the elusive red panda.

I am grateful to God for the brothers and sisters of the International Mission Board, whom I had the privilege of serving for four years. I thank my God every time I remember you, always praying for you with joy because of our partnership in the gospel that transcends any particular position.

I am grateful to God for the members of McLean Bible Church, whom I have the unmerited privilege of pastoring. Let's steward the treasure of God's grace entrusted to us for the spread of God's glory among all nations, beginning right where we live in greater Washington, DC.

I am grateful to God for Chris, Jackie, and the entire Radical team. I am blessed beyond measure to serve the church in accomplishing the mission of Christ alongside you, and I am exhilarated beyond measure about the opportunities that lie before us together.

I am grateful to God for my family. Writing a book is hard, but writing the letter I mentioned near the beginning of this book is infinitely harder. You are more precious to me than words can express. Heather, Caleb, Joshua, Mara, and Isaiah, thank you for the way you love me. Apart from being a child of God, the greatest honor of my life is being your husband and dad.

Most of all, I am grateful to God for the gospel. I have no explanation for why I am writing this book while so many are suffering on the trails I described in this book, many without any knowledge of the gospel. Their faces are continually before me, and I pray that the grace God has granted me might somehow bear fruit for their good and his glory.

"He must increase, but I must decrease" (John 3:30).

# URGENT

## Making Christ known among the unreached

Through Urgent, Radical supports indigenous believers who are making disciples and multiplying healthy churches among the world's hardest to reach people and places.

NORTH KOREA

IRAN

AFGHANISTAN

IRAQ

TIBETANS OF THE HIMALAYAS

SYRIA

BHUTAN

INDIA

LAOS

YEMEN

SOMALIA

SUDAN

LEBANON

## 3.2 billion people

OVER 40% OF THE WORLD'S POPULATION STILL HAVE NEVER HEARD THE GOSPEL.

## INITIATIVES

| Discipleship | Biblical Resources | Humanitarian | Strategy |
|---|---|---|---|
| CHURCH PLANTING | EVANGELISM TOOLS | ANTI-TRAFFICKING EFFORTS | BUSINESS AS MISSIONS |
| TRAINING RESOURCES | LITERATURE DISTRIBUTION | HEALTH-RELATED PROJECTS | AGRICULTURAL AND ENVIRONMENTAL INITIATIVES |
| DISCIPLESHIP TRAINING | TRANSLATION COLLABORATION | | |
| EVANGELISM | | CLEAN WATER INITIATIVES | MOBILIZATION EFFORTS |

## URGENT
### UNITED

Urgent United is a group of individuals united in their purpose of monthly, faithful giving toward an urgent mission.

# urgentneeds.org

A ministry of

# Missions Data Reimagined

The Stratus Index synthesizes reliable data from different sources to clearly display the world's most urgent spiritual and physical needs.

**Identify** country-level needs with nuance and specificity

**Prioritize** areas of high spiritual and physical need

**Match** its resources and expertise to corresponding needs

**Make** informed missional strategies for allocating resources

## More than 30 Data Sources including:

Stratus highlights urgent missional needs by displaying relative rankings of countries rather than raw scores. Rankings update according to applied filters.

Stratus accounts for barriers that have impeded the progress of the gospel. This recalibrated ROI promotes a more equitable distribution of resources where needs are the highest.

" *Stratus aims to address the Great Imbalance by helping the church identify the world's most urgent needs so that it can reallocate its resources more strategically.* "

visit: **stratus.earth**